C000140211

The Porto Aleg.

THE INTERNATIONAL INSTITUTE
FOR RESEARCH AND EDUCATION (IIRE)

Series Editor: PETER DRUCKER

Other titles available

Fatherland or Mother Earth?
Essays on the National Question
Michael Löwy

Understanding the Nazi Genocide
Marxism After Auschwitz
Enzo Traverso

Globalization
Neoliberal Challenge, Radical Responses
Robert Went

-

The Porto Alegre Alternative
Direct Democracy in Action

Edited and translated by Iain Bruce

Pluto  Press

LONDON • ANN ARBOR, MI

with

The International Institute for Research and Education (IIRE)

First published 2004 by Pluto Press
345 Archway Road, London N6 5AA
and 839 Greene Street, Ann Arbor, MI 48106

www.plutobooks.com

Copyright © Iain Bruce and IIRE 2004

The right of the individual contributors to be identified as the authors of
this work has been asserted by them in accordance with the Copyright,
Designs and Patents Act 1988.

British Library Cataloguing in Publication Data
A catalogue record for this book is available from the British Library

ISBN   0 7453 2097 X hardback
ISBN   0 7453 2096 1 paperback

IIRE Notebook for Study and Research no. 35–36

Library of Congress Cataloging in Publication Data applied for

10   9   8   7   6   5   4   3   2   1

Designed and produced for Pluto Press by
Chase Publishing Services, Fortescue, Sidmouth, EX10 9QG, England
Typeset from disk by Stanford DTP Services, Northampton, England
Printed and bound in the European Union by
Antony Rowe Ltd, Chippenham and Eastbourne, England

Contents

List of Tables and Figures

TABLES

FIGURES

IIRE Notebooks for Study and Research

Thousands, even millions of social activists, in trade unions, NGOs, ecological movements, students' and women's organisations, are wrestling with questions about a changing, globalising world. What ended and what began in history when the Berlin Wall fell, and when the global justice movement splashed across the world's TV screens in Seattle? What realistic models can we put forward now in opposition to the reigning neoliberalism? How can we resist neoliberalism's lurking counterparts: nationalism, racism, fundamentalism, communalism?

The International Institute for Research and Education shares these grassroots activists' values: their conviction that societies can and must be changed, democratically, from below, by those who suffer from injustice, on the basis of wide-ranging international solidarity. We exist to help progressives pose the questions and find the answers that they need.

Since 1982 we have welcomed hundreds of participants from over 40 countries to our courses and seminars. Our Ernest Mandel Study Centre, opened in 1995, hosts lectures and conferences on economic and social issues of the post-Cold War world. We have built a network of Fellows who help with these tasks. Our Amsterdam headquarters and library are a resource for researchers and for gatherings of socially minded non-profit groups.

Since 1986 the results of our work – on economic globalisation, twentieth-century history, ecology, feminism, ethnicity, racism, radical movement strategy and other topics – have been made available to a larger public through our monograph series, the Notebooks for Study and Research. The Notebooks are now published in English as books by Pluto Press. Past Notebooks have also been published in other languages, including Arabic, Dutch, French, German, Japanese, Korean, Portuguese, Russian, Spanish, Swedish and Turkish. Back issues of the 20 pre-Pluto Press Notebooks are still available directly from the IIRE.

For information about our publications and other activities, please go to our website – www.iire.org – or write to us: IIRE, Willemsparkweg

202, 1071 HW Amsterdam, Netherlands; email: iire@antenna.nl. Donations to support our work are tax-deductible in several European countries as well as the US.

Acknowledgements

Thanks go to all those who made this book possible, including Eduardo Mancuso, Sandra Jochims, Heloisa Viñola, Jose Brizolla, Assis Brasil, Luciano Brunet, Lucio Costa, Luciana Rodrigues, Andrea Túbero. Special thanks to Peter Drucker at the IIRE and Julie Stoll at Pluto Press, and above all to Maria Esperanza Sanchez and David Bruce.

List of Abbreviations

BARISUL	Publicly owned state bank in Rio Grande do Sul state
CRC	Community Relations Council, coordinates relations between participatory budget and Porto Alegre city hall
CUT	Single Workers' Centre, trade union confederation linked to PT
DS	Socialist Democracy, one of the largest left-wing currents in the PT
FTAA	Free Trade Area of the Americas
GMOs	Genetically modified organisms
IPTU	Buildings tax, most important local source of revenue for municipal governments in Brazil
MDB	Brazilian Democratic Movement, only legal opposition party under the military dictatorship, which later became the Party of the Brazilian Democratic Movement (PMDB)
MOVA	Literacy Movement
MST	Landless Workers' Movement
PB	Participatory budget
PCB	Former Brazilian Communist Party (Moscow-line)
PCdoB	Communist Party of Brazil, largest left party outside the PT, of Maoist origin
PDT	Democratic Party of Labour, populist party in tradition of Getulio Vargas
PT	Brazilian Workers' Party
UAMPA	Union of Neighbourhood Associations of Porto Alegre

Brazil, showing the location of Porto Alegre

Introduction:
From the PT to Porto Alegre

Iain Bruce

This book is about an alternative. It's about an alternative kind of democracy, one that is not limited to electing representatives once every few years and does not assume that freedom is the same thing as consumer choice. It's about an experience of direct democracy in southern Brazil, which for the last decade and a half has been seeking to demonstrate that another world is indeed possible. It's about the system of participatory budgets developed by the Brazilian Workers' Party (PT) in the city of Porto Alegre, which stands in such sharp contrast to the behaviour of the same party since its candidate Luiz Inacio Lula da Silva was elected President of Brazil in 2002.

The origins of that alternative, and this book, go back a long way – to before the birth of the PT a quarter of a century ago.

That is when I first lived in Brazil, in the dying days of the military dictatorship, at the end of the 1970s. Just out of college, for a living I taught English at Itamaraty, the Brazilian Foreign Ministry. For a vocation, I fell in love with Brazil, with Brazilians and with the peculiar combinations of Brazilian politics. The novel approach to democracy that this book deals with has its roots back there, as Brazil prepared to bury two decades of authoritarian military government.

In the end it took the generals some time to pass away. The transition to civilian rule didn't come until 1984. But on the campus at the University of Brasilia, where I'd enrolled as a part-time student, it was already clear that a new period in Brazilian history was beginning. A stream of rallies, occupations and marches, shadowed by military police cordons and occasional tear-gas incursions, fed into a nationwide campaign for a political amnesty for the country's political prisoners and exiles.

After helping to hand out leaflets in the capital's bus station denouncing the arrest and torture of two friends, I found myself, too, briefly detained, threatened, followed by unmarked pick-ups, phoned by unidentified voices, and eventually dismissed from my job at Itamaraty. The policemen who interrogated us shouted angrily about the defence of traditional values and foreign interference. But

1

the tide was moving against them – and it was moving not from without, but from deep within.

That May, a more potent force overtook the campaigns of the students and mainly middle-class opposition. On Friday, 12 May, 2,500 workers on the day shift at the Saab-Scania plant in São Bernardo do Campo clocked on as usual, went to their positions, but refused to switch on their machines. On the Monday 9,500 workers at Ford joined the 'arms-crossed' strike. Within ten days the action had spread to 90 engineering plants across the sprawling industrial belt around São Paulo, known as the ABC. Volkswagen, Mercedes, General Motors and the rest, these motor industry giants that were the precursors of today's corporate globalisation, with their vast factories 30,000 or more workers strong, had engendered an inventive and audacious new trade union movement, which in turn gave birth to a new kind of party, the PT.

One person symbolised this movement. With a ragged beard, unfashionable flares and unbounded charisma – but almost no political baggage – Luis Inacio da Silva, known as Lula, a former machine-tool worker and president of the São Bernardo Metalworkers' Union, was the undisputed figurehead of the strike movement that did more than anything else to hasten the restoration of formal democracy in Brazil.

It wasn't till nearly two years later, when I was back in Europe, commuting between film school in London and my Brazilian girlfriend's doctoral studies in Paris, that the political expression of this movement, the Workers' Party or PT, finally took form – with Lula, of course, as its undisputed leader.

The person who introduced me to that world, and who later played his own part in developing the Porto Alegre experience of participatory democracy, was an impressive example of the other key element that went into forming the PT. Flavio Koutzii had been a member of the Communist Party youth in Rio Grande do Sul and Porto Alegre in the 1960s, alongside Raul Pont, one of the main contributors to this book. He was expelled along with Raul, but then left Brazil. By the early 1970s he was leading one of the guerrilla organisations in Argentina. After several years of imprisonment and horrific torture at the hands of the military government there, he was now in Paris, and like other exiles, coming to terms with his own personal tragedy and the political failures that gave rise to it. Like others of his generation, he was looking for a new way of doing socialist politics. For many long hours he took me painstakingly through the ins and outs of the history of the Brazilian left. But this was never idle reminiscence. Always, there was an underlying sense of purpose – what he and Raul and the others were going to do when they all rejoined forces back in Porto Alegre.

The proposal to launch the PT instantly attracted him and most of Brazil's best left-wing activists. When I met him he was busy organising the 'pro-PT nucleus' in Paris. Of course some old habits died hard. There were at first two separate pro-PT groups in Paris – Flavio's, and another set up by a rival current of the far left. Eventually they fused.

Looking back now, it is not so surprising that this new workers' party – and the system of direct democracy that it later developed in Porto Alegre – came to play 20 years later a part unlike any other in the post-Seattle global justice movement.

For the PT broke the mould that had shaped the international left for more than half a century. In some ways it pointed back to an earlier period. The most important driving force behind the PT was a concentrated factory proletariat not unlike that which gave rise to European workers' parties in the late nineteenth and early twentieth centuries. But it pointed forwards too. Spawned by a new cycle of transnational accumulation, its roots lay not only in the industrial trade unions, but also in a range of other social movements based on the urban poor, the landless peasantry and the dislocated middle classes. Politically, it was the first mass party to emerge from the parallel disappointments of social democracy and Stalinism. The bulk of its activists owed more to Jesus of Nazareth – seen through the lens of liberation theology – than they did to Lenin. The traditional left piled in. But numerically and ideologically, it was always in a minority. Unwittingly, the range of supporters and issues almost prefigured the international movement that was to come. From the earliest days the PT embraced struggles for the emancipation of women, gays and blacks. Campaigns around the debt, intellectual property rights and later genetically modified organisms all fell naturally within its orbit. A decade before Seattle, a Workers' Party leader in the Amazonian state of Acre, Chico Mendes, became an international icon of struggle for the environment, and a symbol of what would later be dubbed the alliance between 'teamsters and turtles'.

But what separated the PT from other big parties of labour around the world was its commitment to democracy – democracy in the broadest and most radical sense. To begin with, that meant democracy within the PT itself. No other party in recent history had brought together several hundred thousand members from the trade unions, from every kind of social movement in both town and country, from the grassroots church communities, from the worlds of academia and the arts, and from every conceivable variant of the organised left, and allowed them all to argue their case, contribute their experience, promote and preserve their own identities, while building a common political project together. The PT encouraged the same kind of plurality within and between the social movements.

Not surprisingly, after two decades of military rule, the PT was deeply committed to defending electoral democracy too. Yet from the start, it also carried with it the dream that another kind of democracy is possible.

It was this peculiar combination of features and visions that made the Brazilian Workers' Party a beacon to the international left back in the 1980s. And to those of us who followed its development over two decades, it was only briefly a surprise to see how that same combination allowed the PT to mesh so easily with the vast and diverse movement for global justice that exploded onto our TV screens at the end of the 1990s.

Indeed it was only then, in the year 2000, that I finally made my first visit to Porto Alegre, and began to see for myself what this peculiar combination had produced on the ground. Over the next few years I returned to the city several times, both for the World Social Forums and to make a documentary about the global justice movement – part of which focused on the participatory budget.

This book deals with the journey between those two points, and the issues raised along the way. Several of the contributions indicate how the system of direct democracy known as the participatory budget emerged in Porto Alegre after 1989 as a largely unplanned synthesis. Part I draws on extended interviews with some of the key protagonists to tell the story of how this synthesis developed. It explains how the concerns of the community movement found voice in the new democratic space opened up by the end of Brazil's military dictatorship. These concerns intersected with the assorted dreams and programmes of the Brazilian left, almost all of them expressed through the PT itself.

In Part II, Ubiratan de Souza, André Passos, Pepe Vargas and Edinho Silva explain and interpret the way this synthesis works in practice. They also touch, directly or indirectly, on the international context in which the participatory budget emerged – marked by that emblematic date 1989, the year when the paradigms of 'actually existing socialism' came tumbling down and history was said to have come to an end, when the institutions of the marketplace and representative democracy were consecrated as the best of all possible arrangements in the best of all possible worlds.

In Part III, Raul Pont and João Machado take a longer, more theoretical view of the participatory budget as the germ of an alternative vision and an alternative practice, as a key constituent part of an emerging conviction that 'another world is possible'.[1]

The heart of this book is to be found in these chapters, where key architects and practitioners give their own account of how the participatory budget developed, how it works and what it means. Before that, in Chapter 1, I try to locate the participatory budget within some of the strategic debates raised by the global justice movement, and begin to explain just why its strengths and limitations matter so much to all those who identify with the aspirations of that movement.

But first, the Prologue aims to give a flavour of what it feels like for the men and women of Porto Alegre to take control over how their city's money is spent.

This book does not try to deal with the record of the Lula government in Brasilia. This has been a testing experience for the Brazilian left, and indirectly for the global justice movement too. Some would say it has been a traumatic one. For the present purposes, it may be enough to point to the huge gulf between what this book tells us of the PT's practice in Porto Alegre – its ability to combine pragmatic flexibility with radical innovation and creativity – and the troubling failure of nerve and vision that marked the PT's federal administration after January 2003.

Prologue: The View from Below

It's the day before the big budget meeting in Gloria. Local community activists have been busy all week with preparations. Is everything sorted out with the Dom Pedro I school where the assembly will be held? Have the people in Maraba booked their own coaches? Who's going to do the final flyer posting in Rincão?

Gloria is one of Porto Alegre's 16 regions. After a series of smaller, less formal meetings in individual neighbourhoods, tomorrow's annual assembly is the chance for all Gloria residents to debate and decide their priorities for next year's local government budget. Do they want public spending to concentrate on building houses or putting in sewers, on paving the roads or providing health centres and schools? For the people of this region, the open assembly will be the centrepiece of an innovation in local democracy that has made their city famous around the world. For this is Porto Alegre's participatory budget.

The name may be inelegant, but for a decade and a half the participatory budget has been examined, debated, and copied – sometimes caricatured – by community movements and local governments across Latin America and in other parts of the world. The basic idea is simple and radical. It is to transfer the power to decide how the city's money is spent, away from the technocrats in City Hall and the elected politicians in the council chamber and into the hands of the population, meeting in open public assemblies like the one being prepared here in Gloria.

This part of Porto Alegre has a rich history of community organisation. The network of neighbourhood associations here goes back to the time of resistance to the military dictatorship that ruled Brazil from 1964 to 1984. The organisations here played an active part in introducing the participatory budget after the Brazilian Workers' Party (PT) first won the elections for the city's mayor in 1988. But there are still areas of Gloria that have barely been touched by the processes of participatory democracy.

I've just come back from visiting Dona Veva, a shantytown perched on a hillside that has a reputation for drugs and night-time gang violence. I went with Heloisa, a local community activist, and Sandra, the city council's fulltime liaison person for the Gloria region. The journey itself was an illustration of what Porto Alegre's participatory budget, or PB, has and has not achieved.

We travelled on one of the city's smart new buses. They tell me Porto Alegre now has the best public transport system in Brazil. It's been achieved, they hasten to add, not through privatisation, but through building up the existing, publicly owned bus company into a well-equipped, efficiently run model, whose standards of service all the other private concessionaires are obliged to emulate. We travelled through the winding suburbs of the city's outer periphery on a road that had been freshly tarmacked. They tell me this has been the single most constant priority set by the PB over the last 15 years. Made-up roads and paved streets make a big difference here. Much more than Rio de Janeiro or São Paulo, Porto Alegre is a city of open, half-rural spaces. The poor neighbourhoods and 'illegal' land occupations that house many of those forced to flee the countryside are widely spread. Decent roads and streets are not only a prerequisite for drains, sanitation and the rest of the missing urban infrastructure; they are also essential to let the buses in. And without buses you can't even begin to go and look for work.

Dona Veva itself is closer to the Rio image of a favela high above the city. From the end of the paved road where the bus stops, a smart new stone stairway leads straight up the hillside to the first group of shacks. Round the corner, the stairway heads up further to the rest of the shantytown. But that's as far as the participatory budget has got in Dona Veva.

A group of residents explains to Sandra that their main problem is the lack of functioning drains and an open rubbish tip. When it rains, the drains get blocked and the tip overflows. Household waste, and worse, spills out all over the place. Heloisa asks if they know about the PB. Yes, they know the PB built the stairway and sorted out the buses, but that's not enough.

Heloisa and Sandra begin to explain that if they only get a group together and go along to tomorrow's budget meeting, they'll be able to vote for sanitation as their top priority for the Gloria region. And for every ten of them that go along, they'll be able to elect one delegate, whose job it will then be to make sure that priority gets translated into the drains and rubbish disposal they need right here. They nod and say they'll try and get to the meeting. But the truth is they look a bit sceptical.

I didn't see any of them at the budget assembly the following evening. Maybe that's because it was raining hard. They were probably too busy trying to unblock their drains.

Tonight, however, the southern winter still seems some way off. The activists are worried that the forecast of rain might affect tomorrow's turnout. They've been hoping for more than the 800 or so they had at last year's PB assembly. But for the time being, as we gather to discuss their experience of 15 years of the participatory budget, the autumn air is sticky. A fan whirs noisily in the corner of a bare room in the local government's regional office. I ask the six of them – all local community leaders and activists[1] – what they see as the strong and weak points of the participatory budget so far.

JOSE: I think the strong points are the way the community organises and decides on public resources democratically, by participating. That's one of the main positive points. It's turned around the way Porto Alegre's people make their demands. Before the popular administration came in, demands were made through the council chamber and the mayor's office. But not now. Now there's direct, popular participation, which decides where and how public investments should be made and oversees the entire process through to completion. So that's the positive side. The main weakness I would say is that you can't get the resources you need to do everything at once. The communities are anxious to carry out as many projects as possible, but there aren't enough resources.

SIRLEY: I think Brizola's right because all the areas of Gloria, including my own, which includes six micro-areas, gained a great deal. At the beginning for example the roads were in a terrible state. Now they've been made up and extended. There's lighting. All this was very positive for those of us who live in the so-called periphery, and we agree there's been a huge step forwards. However as Brizola says there are also some limitations. For example the community gets involved so long as they're gaining something. As soon as they stop gaining, the participation can dry up. So we can see how difficult it is to bring people from outside into the community organisations. People go along thinking they'll see immediate results. But the process is a long one. In spite of its being democratic, you don't necessarily get what you want first time or second time. So those of us in the community organisations feel that if we don't win anything this year then we'll be discredited next year. Since city hall doesn't have a big apparatus, we end up doing all the work. Then when the criteria are applied and our project doesn't come off, all that mobilisation we've spent a year building up simply collapses. And after that it's very difficult to get those people back together again. But still, it's a popular, democratic local government, and previous local governments never did anything like that. So we still believe in it. We still think that through participation we can achieve many more things. But we would like more incentives from the local government bodies.

HELOISA: The thing Sirley mentions is something that weakens the movement. People go and fight for their own particular project. Once they win that, they leave. They don't continue fighting for the rest of the community, for the neighbourhood as a whole, for overall improvements. They go along because they want their street paved. Once they get their street paved, they're not interested in the children without a creche; they disappear. So that weakens the movement. And this is a job the popular movement needs to tackle, not the PB itself. You mobilise people but they're only interested in their own interests, in gazing at their own navels, not in the collective interest. The PB has to function on the basis of collective interests and it's the popular movement's job to promote this collective spirit, to fight for the good of all and not for particular interests.

JOSE: We're also looking at the way the movement is organised. We don't think the PB should control the whole process in the community. There should be more coming from the popular organisations. The way it's been going over the last 15 years or so, I think there's been a period of paralysis for the community organisations, where everything was being decided through the PB bodies and the popular movement ended up being weakened. So I think one of the negative points is this question of the popular movement.

SILVIO: In my opinion the most important thing the PB has brought to the whole population is the question of popular participation. When it began 15 years ago, in a very different political situation, which all of us can remember to some extent, the people were mere spectators. There was a lot of paternalism on the part of many politicians, who carried out public works as a way of winning support for their own interests, not those of the community. With the arrival of the PB people began to become protagonists of political change. By organising themselves they began to see the changes – sewage, paving – and I think it's an example of popular participation for the whole world. People have become agents of change. Change, transformation, are for me the best words to define the PB.

You talk about change. What's the most important aspect? The changes gained in terms of concrete benefits – paving, health care and so on – or the political change in terms of people's participation?

JOSE: I think it's the political aspect. It wasn't just the mayor's office that started the PB on its own, out of good will, because it had an ideological commitment to popular participation. It was the independent popular movement too. This region, Gloria, for example, already had an independent People's Council in existence before the PB came into existence. So for us the PB started as a sub-committee of the Gloria People's Council. It was this autonomous popular movement that initiated the PB in Porto Alegre, which resulted in the Workers' Party (PT) being re-elected for four consecutive mandates. To this day we have a strong People's Council here in Gloria, where we discuss right across our region what we want and organise to make it happen. So I think this political question is the key aspect. Heloisa is right when she says that people come to the PB to fight for their own street, for their own little area...

SIRLEY: Because they want health facilities, housing...

JOSE: For particular things to do with one street rather than the whole community. But many of them then realise that they have to fight for the whole region. So for example, I come along to get a certain thing fixed in my street, but then I discover there are all those families over there going hungry, so maybe I should vote for social services. Or I'm fighting for my street to be paved but then there's an eviction going on – maybe housing should be the priority. So that's the kind of political growth there's been.

HELOISA: That's right. People do often go along on behalf of their own street, to get their project passed. But when they get there they learn the meaning of solidarity. They see that if they fight for the whole community, they come out winners and the whole community comes out winners too.

But for ordinary people, aren't the concrete things the important ones?

NILVEN: I think there are various things. There's paving the streets and other public works for the poorest sections of our community, especially those living in the favelas up on the hills. These are things we go out into the neighbourhoods to work for, things we come to the PB to demand. I think we need to be more and more united behind this effort to change the reality of our communities, which is none too good here in the city or anywhere in Brazil. But there are also social issues like drugs, which are also an aspect of this reality, which tear families apart every day. This is a particular concern for me. So we're using the PB to demand better social services for drug users, to ensure a space for them, so that they can find a way back to being people who participate fully in our community. All this is part of the movement. It's not just about asphalt and streetlights. There's also the human aspect.

SIRLEY: The different things come together. Because people don't just need social services but also housing, healthcare...

NILVEN: All these things are important. And the participation of the community as a whole is the most important thing of all. We feel that our participation is a part of this development of the whole community. This is what the PB represents.

SILVIO: That's the spirit of citizenship. The PB was set up in a context where the community was completely abandoned, where everything was lacking, where education and public services were in a state of ruin. The PB emerged as a project where the community, out of this daily experience of walking through the mud and filth, without schools, and with all the other difficulties, became the agent of change.

EDIMAR: Before the community did mobilise, but the projects were decided on in the council chamber, behind closed doors. Now they know what the community is demanding. They don't just imagine what the community might need; they have to follow what particular communities are demanding. It changes people's attitude towards politics. Before they'd just go 'Nah! That's just politics, just party stuff.' But now they begin to fight, and they realise that if they want a particular thing they need to get involved, politics or not. So poor people, who didn't have much knowledge, begin to understand how things work and get more involved in the movement, first to win something for themselves but also to help others. So they learn a sense of solidarity.

There are examples like Katia, a woman who'd never been to school. She couldn't even write her name. She began to take an active part, and as a result she then went back to study, because she decided she needed to.

HELOISA: Someone like that begins to take part, begins to see that her ideas are accepted by the movement and by the local government, and that creates the self-esteem she needs to believe in herself again, to struggle for what she wants, improve her own life too, and help the community as a whole.

But some critics say it's a fictitious democracy, that it's manipulated, because the PB ends up just approving policies that have already been decided by the town hall...

JOSE: I disagree...

SILVIO: I disagree too...

JOSE: I disagree because, when the PB began, I was one of the first PB councillors, and I can tell you that we built this. It didn't exist. I remember in 1988, when we began to discuss it, we had the mayor, all the secretaries and 16 councillors in the plenary meetings. And we began to see how we'd do it. So we built this budget. There was no model, no handbook, no instruction manual on how to do it. No, we built it up ourselves. And from the moment the people built it, they began to govern too; they became co-government.

If citizenship is one of the most important things, this participatory budget has created citizens; it has turned so many people into conscious citizens. For example, in the early years, what did the people of Porto Alegre choose as their top priority? Paving their streets. Issues of social services, land ownership, healthcare and education were never in first place. Today they are. That shows that people's awareness as citizens has grown. That's something we've built.

Another important aspect is that this budget is not law. It's not fixed. It's something that is in permanent discussion and development. I have some serious questions – this is an important battle we're having at the moment – about the need to develop the PB further. I think we can take it further. I don't think the PB process is anywhere near its limits.

Go further how?

JOSE: For me the big step would be to go beyond discussing just the city's income and public works. We need to discuss the budget as a whole. We need to discuss local services, the policy on services. At the moment it's just the policy on capital investment that gets discussed. All spending on capital investment is up for discussion, but not the issue of services. At the moment 65 per cent of the council's income goes to pay the council workforce. But society has no control over this wage bill. This has to change. The PB has to include capital investment AND services. That's a struggle we have at the moment. If we don't move forward on this, the PB will run out of steam, and may even go backwards.

HELOISA: With what we've got the community manages to control and supervise where its own money is invested. And now we want to control the part that's spent on services too. We want to check whether that money's being well-spent or whether it could be better spent elsewhere.

SILVIO: Exactly. The PB isn't a closed box that you can't put anything into or take anything out of. On the contrary it's permanently changing and moving forward. The proposals made by our community here in Gloria are considered by the whole of the city. That's the big advantage of the PB, in my opinion. It's always developing. It's up to the community itself to make a judgement, and decide what changes to make. It's the community that's involved on the ground, that knows what's happening, that can see where the problems lie and come up with alternatives. That's one of the most positive things about the PB. It's a participatory democracy that was built by the community, and is still being built by the community. It's an open process, in permanent flux, which makes it very difficult for anyone to manipulate it. As far as the problem raised by Heloisa is concerned, I think it's true. People go along to get their sewers or their creche, and then disappear from the participatory budget. This leads to demobilisation in their own communities. And to get those people involved again – because mobilisation is the real secret of the PB – is quite difficult. Maybe that's why some people talk about manipulation. Because the community that doesn't have sewers or doesn't have a creche, mobilises and gets 100 or 200 people along to the PB assembly. And any community that doesn't mobilise gets left behind. So it's all down to the community. They are the ones who have to get organised and take their people along.

NILVEN: It's through the community's participation that the PB's achievements are won. If there weren't that participation, then as Silvio says there might be manipulation. But in fact it's not manipulation, it's just greater involvement on the part of certain communities.

HELOISA: The PB also has the advantage that if any leader gets elected, does the work, and then lets the power go to his or her head, then the community will be ready to remove that person just as quickly. The community is no longer willing to be cheated, because people have learnt to struggle and have their say. So people come along and try to manipulate the PB, they get very short shrift from the community. Either they don't get re-elected, or they have their mandate revoked. They lose their power.

EDIMAR: The fact is we govern without being the government. We govern...

HELOISA: ... collectively.

EDIMAR: That's right, collectively. So some leader might go along and sign in the name of the government. But if that's not what we want, then we say that's not right, we want it this other way. We're the ones who put you there, so go and do it the way we want. We gave the government its power, so it'll have to follow our instructions.

If it were possible to get all aspects of public works, payroll and services included in the PB, wouldn't that still be far from enough to deal with the big problems of poverty and inequality that face people in Brazil?

HELOISA: That would require a PB on a national scale. Because poverty is the result of national policies. There's no way a municipality can solve that sort of problem.

SILVIO: Rio Grande do Sul and Porto Alegre, home of the World Social Forum, are part of the wider context. The same thing obviously goes for the participatory budget. We live in Brazil, which has been the target of a neoliberal project that almost everyone here in Rio Grande do Sul condemns, because it offers no progress in terms of social policies. It just creates more poverty. But that's beyond the control of the city or state, beyond the control of the community. This certainly prevents the PB from making more rapid progress. It's the general political context. Yet the example of Porto Alegre and, for a time, Rio Grande do Sul state, has still been an inspiration for the whole world and a proposal, a dream, a utopia, for Brazil itself.

JOSE: What Silvio says is definitely right. We cannot imagine that Porto Alegre is an island separate from the wider world. The neoliberal policy of globalisation comes from the top down, and we're in the middle. Brazil, as a part of Latin America, is part of the poor world. It's not part of the G7. Brazil today is still regarded as a colony. This is a context we cannot get away from.

However this IS a seed. It shows there ARE alternatives, that there is a way out. And in this big social movements like the Landless Workers' Movement (MST), which is also working for an alternative, support us. The MST can combine its alternative with the alternative of the participatory budget, so that at least public spending can be more fully discussed and directed to meet social needs. Where did public money go before? The same place the federal government's budget went to – to rescue the banks and the big bankers. But not here in Porto Alegre. Here the money is invested in projects that benefit the community.

HELOISA: Citizens have learnt with the PB how to fight for their interests without resorting to violence. They can get what they want without screaming and breaking things. They've learnt there's a space where they can go and argue with the government, say look this street here's no good, that project there won't work, you'll have to reroute the other. And often it is the community that comes up with the best route, because the technicians don't know exactly what the community needs. So citizens have learnt they have a right not only to fight for their demands, but a right to have their own vision of how things work, and to insist on the things that improve the whole situation.

But obviously that still falls far short of being able to cope with the whole international context.

JOSE: Of course that's right. The participatory budget is not going to save the world. Let's be absolutely clear about that. It's a question of improving public investments.

HELOISA: And giving people the power to oversee those improvements.

JOSE: Now for me the big problem in Brazil is the foreign debt. The big problem for the state is the huge hole left after paying millions and millions a month on the foreign debt. This can only be dealt with through a moratorium, or I don't know what. But there has to be a way out of this.

HELOISA: The money just goes to support the rich countries. It's our cheap labour benefiting the rich countries. We have to export everything cheaply. They make laws to protect their own products, and our products lose out.

SILVIO: This is something else it's worth bringing out about the PB. Because people don't just stop at the end of their street, with the concerns of their own neighbourhood. The whole time we find our discussions running into international issues that affect us too. The question of FTAA for example – the Free Trade Area of the Americas. I'm against. I don't think we are slaves. They try to make out that Brazilians are illiterate, that this is the land of football and samba. But on the contrary, I think that the PB, along with the MST, shows that we have an alternative. It may not be perfect. But it is an alternative that fights against social exclusion. There's so much poverty in the world today. Yet at the same time there are so many examples of communities struggling, showing that it is possible to fight against exclusion, hunger, poverty and illiteracy. And Rio Grande do Sul is playing an important part in this. Why? Is it because of the government? No, it's because of us. We're the ones who built this, who are concerned about our communities, about our children.

NILVEN: Silvio mentioned illiteracy. Here in Porto Alegre we have the MOVA, the Literacy Movement – I'm one of the teachers. It's a real joy to see pupils of mine, 70 or 80 years old, who'd never picked up a pen in their lives, who can now read, write their names, and don't have to rely on someone else to tell them if this is the bus that goes past their home. All this is part of our movement, which comes down to valuing human beings in all their aspects. People who'd never had the opportunity to study now do. They're no longer shut up at home waiting to die. It's a question of self-esteem. And of hope.

JOSE: So the PB gets people thinking about things big and small, from the 80-year-old who wants to learn to read and write to the issue of free trade in the Americas. The key thing for me about any social revolution is that it has to start from citizens who are...

HELOISA: ... committed.

JOSE: Committed and well-informed, aware of reality. So that's what the PB is proposing. More than just public works, it manages to discuss the big issues. And I don't believe in any revolution that doesn't start with conscious, aware citizens. It may only be a grain of sand on a very big beach, but these grains of sand are multiplying. If only we can spread this, as it has been up at the state level, in spite of all the difficulties we had there with the kind of right wing we faced in the State Assembly. That meant the PB had to be implemented by the people themselves and not by the state government because the resources weren't released. I mean just imagine what the left's victory in the presidential elections could mean! The PB should be implemented across Brazil. I think this is a model that the WORLD needs. Because the world today is in a situation...

NILVEN: ... It's so individualistic.

JOSE: If globalisation continues the way it is now, we'll reach a point where half a dozen powerful people decide everything in the world. And that's bad for everyone.

SILVIO: If we're going to get into the whole question of capitalism and what path the country should follow, then I would say that the participatory budget serves workers like us. In fact, for us workers this is probably the best option of all, because it's enabled us to regain our self-esteem, it's made us full citizens. In fact, it's made us realise that we ARE important.

HELOISA: And it's made us realise that bringing people together isn't just a slogan to shout in the streets – you know that one, 'The people united [will never be defeated].' It's something we can actually do, not just shout about.

JOSE: Look, Brazil is the world's eighth biggest economy. So how can a third of the country's population be going hungry? Something is obviously going wrong. That's what begins to come out of these discussions, not only in the PB but also in the neighbourhood associations, in the unions, in the MST.

Here in Porto Alegre you've become something of a reference point, a symbol, for the international movement against globalisation. How do you feel about that?

NILVEN: I personally feel very good about that. Because I feel good about the work we're doing here, and I'd like that to be an example for others. And it comes out of little things. For example, a few days ago there was a storm and several families in our neighbourhood lost their homes. Through city hall we managed to get three houses for them. I get very emotional when I think about the significance of things like this that we can achieve through the PB, through participation.

SIRLEY: Being an example around the world, being held up as a model, has actually made us *more* participatory. It's encouraged us to go further. We are proud we can say to the world that here, in a country like this, in Porto Alegre, in Brazil, in America, it's the community that's in charge. It's the community that points the way, and the government that follows. We don't depend any more on local city councillors, who cheat us by saying that our street will benefit only if we vote for them. Now we are the ones the city councillors depend on. Now they are our employees. It's their job to approve the spending that we've decided on. We are the ones who decide what the priorities are. We say which areas the money should go to and which particular works the money should be spent on. That's really important for us. We began burrowing away at really local stuff like that, and now that's given us the confidence and the authority to speak about free trade in the Americas, the World Social Forum and global issues of health and housing, and to become an example for the rest of the world. That's something we could never have imagined before. So yes, we want to send this message to people around the world so that they can take these advances further... in countries that haven't been involved yet.

HELOISA: And in other cities too. We began small. But if every small town and city can become aware of the power that each citizen has, then we may not solve all the world's problems, but we can solve quite a few of them. And most importantly we can help those people to become aware of what they're doing. In that way, corruption and misuse of public money are reduced. Because the people are always present. When someone offers a bribe to the mayor or a city councillor, he or she knows that there's someone watching what money comes in and what money goes out. The people are overseeing the work. They know what is expected and how much it's supposed to cost. If there's a grain of sand missing, they'll know. The community doesn't just demand such and such a project. It oversees every stage of the process, right through to completion and beyond. It's something people have won for themselves. It's not something some city councillor has given them because he wants to look good. It's like their own child, so they value it and make sure it will be well cared for in the future too.

SILVIO: I think what we're doing here is sowing a seed. It's a seed we've planted, watered and watched over every day. Now it's growing, strong and pretty. But it needs attention too. You have to prune back the branches so it can grow stronger. Like a mother watching her child grow up healthy and sound, of course we too are happy to see this seed of ours growing, gathering more support. One thing I'm certain of – I don't know if I can speak for everyone here – is that the participatory budget is here to stay. But it's important to add that this is something that is permanently under construction. It's not a closed process. It's not done and dusted. It's the community's great achievement. It's a way of combating poverty, of bringing improvements, of countering social exclusion.

The world today is experiencing a huge social collapse. Here in Rio Grande do Sul we've been reversing this, through the PB. People get to live with more dignity. They get more access to food, to education, basic sanitation, and decent streets, all through the PB. If this is an example for the rest of the world, so be it. Let them come to Porto Alegre.

JOSE: Of course our state of Rio Grande do Sul was already a reference point for democratic movements in the past. Before the military dictatorship, this was the strongest base for the popular movement, throughout the early 1960s and right up until the military coup came to put a stop to all that in 1964. So Porto Alegre has a tradition of democracy and participation. We have a strong MST here; we have strong trade unions and neighbourhood organisations. All of this is what made it possible for the PB to develop into what it is today.

However I still don't think the PB is some sort of salvation for this country. In fact much of the PB's strength comes from the fact that it IS still under construction. We still haven't achieved 10, 20, 30 per cent of what the PB is capable of. I think we'll only get close to the limits of what is possible with the PB – I say close because the sky is the final limit – when we manage to make the whole population aware that this is part of something much bigger. When people understand that what we're fighting for now, here in our neighbourhood, in our region, here in Porto Alegre, here in our state, is part of a bigger whole. And in the end we'll have to get to that whole, to the countries led by this G7 for example. We'll have to take on those 200 global companies that control more than 60 per cent of all the wealth in the world. These are the things we're going to have to take on. And I think that's where this tremendous growth of citizenship that's happening through the participatory budget is heading. Our reference point can't just be whether or not our streets have been paved; it can't just be about ensuring that public money goes where people want it to go and isn't siphoned off into some private slush fund. We have to aim much higher. That's why we've been developing this for 15 years here in Porto Alegre, for four years at state level, and now have at least the possibility of implementing it in the whole of Brazil. If we can't do that, if we don't replant this seed of ours constantly, at every level, then I really don't know what will happen to this country, and to this world of ours.

Part I

The Participatory Budget –
Origins, Aims and Ambiguities

1
Participatory Democracy – The Debate

Iain Bruce

There is a contradiction at the heart of Porto Alegre's participatory budget. It is a contradiction shared, by implication, with the global justice movement that made Porto Alegre its first home. How can it be that the most radical experiment in direct democracy for decades – an experiment consciously inspired by the Paris Commune and the early Russian soviets, the sharpest challenge yet to prevailing identifications of democracy with the institutions of parliamentary representation – has developed, peacefully, within the constitutional framework of a dependent capitalist country like Brazil? If the participatory budget is indeed the seed of another possible world, why has it lain so long in the ground, without much to indicate that such a spectacular new plant was about to blossom?

You can put the same question in different ways. How has the PB become an obligatory reference for both the radical left and the new right within Brazil's governing Workers' Party? How can a site of devotion for the left in the global justice movement – the main reason for Porto Alegre being chosen to host the first three World Social Forums – also be an object of praise for the United Nations' Habitat and even the World Bank? How can it be that Porto Alegre provides a model for local governments of very different hues across Latin America and beyond – including not only the most inventive and radical amongst them, but also several from the old-fashioned, social-democratic centre-left and others of the third-way centre-right? How can the participatory budget be all things to all people?

This contradiction overlaps with several broader ambiguities, ambiguities that intensified in the closing years of the last century and remain amongst the greatest challenges facing the politics of emancipation in the early years of this one. These ambiguities, about the meaning of 'community', 'participation' and 'power', and about the connection between 'democracy' and 'socialism', were of course present long before the fall of the Berlin Wall. But they have taken on greater importance since then. Addressing them is an inescapable task for those seeking to restate the case for socialism in the twenty-first century, in an idiom that makes sense to the new generations coming to politics after Seattle and the immense movement against war in Iraq.

DILEMMAS OF A LULA GOVERNMENT

The most immediate manifestation of this contradiction is the strategic dilemma that faced the Brazilian Workers' Party when its candidate, Luis Inacio Lula da Silva, donned the presidential sash in Brasilia on 1 January 2003. Clearly there have been very different views of this challenge, then and since, both outside and inside the PT, and even within the PT government itself. To a considerable extent these different views can be seen as projections of different attitudes that had been developing to the PT's earlier experiences in local government – to what had become known in party circles as 'the PT way of governing' ('o modo petista de governar').

Everyone in the PT accepted that the participatory budget had become a key component of this 'PT way of governing'. For many, especially on the left of the party, it was *the* defining characteristic of the PT's experience at the local level. As such, it was an indispensable pointer to how a PT government at the national level should approach its tasks. Several months before Brazil's presidential elections in October 2002, the former mayor of Porto Alegre, and one of the main contributors to this book, Raul Pont,[1] told me how he saw the challenge:

> Participatory democracy has to be a central part of the PT's programme. Here in Brazil, the existing institutions of representative democracy are designed to consolidate social inequalities, bureaucracy and corruption. If Lula wins the presidency he'll have only a small minority in Congress. In that situation, the participatory budget, having a direct relationship with the people, becomes a life and death necessity. If Lula doesn't adopt mechanisms like this to rule the country, he'll remain a hostage to Congress. He won't rule. His government will be a government of the conservative majority in Congress; it won't be ours. This is a crossroads for the PT and for the left in Brazil.

The majority of the PT's leaders, however, had a different view. They too made repeated reference to the need for 'participatory democracy'. The Guidelines for a Governmental Programme, which they adopted at the last party conference before the elections at the end of 2001 in the northeastern city of Recife, even spoke of the 'tremendous challenge' of implementing the participatory budget at national level.

But once in the presidential palace, the steps taken were very modest. The main initiative was to set up a Council of Economic and Social Development – led by another former Porto Alegre mayor, Tarso Genro, from the party's political centre ground – to 'advise' the president. With 82 nominated members, including 29 representatives of industry, commerce and agribusiness, seven bankers, 13 trade unionists (several of these from the pro-business union confederations), one representative of the Landless Workers' Movement (MST) and four or five from other social movements, this Council was intended to channel suggestions from civil society into government policy. But both its composition and its lack of real power suggested it had more to do with cementing the new government's pact with the business community than with handing control to the population.

A few months later the government organised 27 public consultation meetings in Brazil's various states to discuss the 'Multi-Year Plan'. But again the breadth of popular participation was restricted, and the powers purely consultative.

The fact that *The Economist* of London, which was already heaping praise on the Lula government for its adherence to ultra-orthodox macroeconomic policies, could hail such initiatives as examples of the PT government's commitment to democratic participation in policymaking shows just how wide the potential gap is between this neoliberal view of participatory democracy and the radical version envisaged by Raul Pont.

WHERE THE DIFFERENCES CAME FROM

These quite different views of 'the PT way of governing' go back a long way – to the very origins of the PT and its component parts. However, they have become slowly clearer since the early years of the 1980s when the PT elected its first local governments.

In 1982 the PT elected its first mayor in Diadema, one of the industrial suburbs around São Paulo. Brazil was still under military rule; the PT, just two years old, was still very much the political expression of the huge wave of strikes that was hastening the dictatorship's demise. Diadema was one of the areas where the strike movement had been strongest. In 1985, with the military gone and democratic elections finally extended to state capitals,[2] the PT added Fortaleza, the capital city of the northeastern state of Ceara. It was the diocesan seat of one of Brazil's most radical bishops and hence a strong base for the movement of grassroots church communities inspired by liberation theology. Symbolically then, these two locations represented two of the three main components that had come together to found the Workers' Party in 1980: the new industrial working class and the radical Catholic Church.

It was only after the 1988 local elections, however, that the PT really made its mark in local government. This time it occupied the mayor's office in 36 towns and cities across Brazil, most importantly in the state capitals São Paulo and Porto Alegre. The experience of the first PT administration in São Paulo, Brazil's biggest city, ended up being a mixed one. The party failed to win re-election there in 1992. It was Porto Alegre that became the standardbearer for the PT's achievements in local government. The PT won re-election there not only in 1992 but again in 1996 and in 2000. Partly on the strength of this record, in 1998 the PT won the wider state elections for governor and vice-governor of Rio Grande do Sul, of which Porto Alegre is the capital.

Porto Alegre, with a population of nearly 1.4 million, is not a major industrial centre. The trade union presence in the local PT was significant, but came mainly from the public sector and services like banks. Olívio Dutra, the first PT mayor of Porto Alegre and later the first PT governor of Rio Grande do Sul, was himself a former leader of the bank workers' union. More important, especially for the development of the participatory budget, was the powerful movement of community organisations, which owed much to the grassroots 'church of the poor'.[3] However, Porto Alegre also had an abundant supply of the third main component that went into the formation of the Workers' Party: the organised Marxist left.[4]

ORGANISED LEFT CURRENTS

From its inception, the PT had included a number of organised currents coming from the various strands of the traditional left, by and large those which at different times and on different ideological grounds had broken with the old Moscow-line Brazilian Communist Party (the PCB or *'partidão'*). In the late 1960s and early 1970s, many of these currents had been involved in disastrous attempts at armed struggle against the military dictatorship.

For example the PT president at the start of the Lula presidency, José Genoino Neto, had taken part in a rural guerrilla campaign organised in the early 1970s by the Communist Party of Brazil (PCdoB)[5] in the Amazon region of Araguaia. He was one of the very few survivors. He later split from that party before taking his supporters into the recently formed PT. The previous party president, President Lula's first chief of staff and the *éminence grise* behind the new PT government, José Dirceu, was a student leader who became involved with the urban guerrilla movement at the end of the 1960s. Imprisoned by the military regime, he was one of the prisoners exchanged for kidnapped US Ambassador Charles Elbrick in 1969. He spent part of his exile in Cuba before undergoing plastic surgery and returning to live clandestinely in a small town in Parana state. He joined the PT with a group of other former members and sympathisers of the urban guerrilla movement whose political education and affinities lay close to the leaders of the Cuban revolution.[6] Several other senior figures in the Lula government, like influential Finance Minister Antonio Palocci, came to the PT from strands of the Trotskyist tradition.[7]

Two important points emerge from these often convoluted, sometimes dramatic, personal histories. First, whatever their ideological roots, from the beginning all these left currents of the PT agreed on the absolute primacy of democratic struggle. This was a natural consequence of the defeat of the Cuban guerrilla model and the rise of mass democratic struggles against the military dictatorship – democratic struggles that were being led by the other two main components in the PT's formation, the trade unionists around Lula and the radical Catholic Church.

Second, although many of these left currents soon broke up or disappeared as organised forces, their origins continued to inform significantly different *approaches* to the democratic struggle. We can see these different approaches, along with a number of other influences, feeding later into different understandings of the 'PT way of governing' and the participatory budget.

SOCIALIST DEMOCRACY

This can be seen from the particular example of the left current that has been most important in the PT in Porto Alegre and in

Rio Grande do Sul state, and which has been the main driving force behind the participatory budget there: the Socialist Democracy tendency (DS).[8]

DS was formed *in the process* of preparing the founding of the PT. It saw itself as an integral part of the new party, which it said it wanted to help develop into a revolutionary party. Indeed it had a prolonged debate with the other organised left currents in the PT, and particularly with the group around José Genoino, all of whom saw the PT as a temporary, tactical front whilst they themselves represented the true revolutionary project. Flowing directly out of this discussion, DS conducted another lengthy and ultimately successful campaign to give the PT's internal organisation the large measure of democracy that distinguished it for so long. This included the right to form political tendencies within the party, proportional representation for minority viewpoints on the PT leadership, and a minimum quota for women on those same leadership bodies.

DS also had something of an obsession with the wider relationship between socialism and democracy. The international current with which DS identified had a long history of opposition to the bureaucratic and authoritarian character of Stalinist regimes. In the same year in which DS began to come together, 1979, it was engaged in a new discussion about the nature of socialist democracy. Partly this was an attempt to formulate a revolutionary response to the turn by many West European communist parties to wholehearted endorsement of the parliamentary road to socialism and the virtues of representative democracy. This turn – referred to at the time as 'Eurocommunism' – had itself produced some interesting experiences in local government. The Italian Communist Party's administration of 'Red Bologna' in the 1970s, for example, has been compared with the PT administration in Porto Alegre. In fact, as we shall see, there are significant differences, and some of these relate to the rather different perspective on socialist democracy being developed by DS.

DS and its international partners had little to say initially about combining direct democracy with parliamentary institutions. At first they attempted instead to introduce the principles of multiparty democracy and universal suffrage into a traditional Marxist scheme of direct, council or soviet democracy. However, 1979 was also the year of the Sandinista revolution in Nicaragua. When the Sandinistas moved away from reliance on a form of direct representation through the Council of State in the early 1980s and called multiparty elections to a National Assembly, DS's earlier discussion on socialist democracy moved one step further forward. Many on the revolutionary left in Latin America and elsewhere lamented the Sandinistas' move as a concession to 'bourgeois institutions'. DS and its co-thinkers, however, welcomed the move as a practical demonstration – the first of its kind in recent history – that revolution and the ballot box, far from being incompatible, were a desirable combination.[9]

But of course it was in Porto Alegre itself, with the PT administration's attempts to develop participatory democracy after 1989, that DS's new thinking about socialist democracy found a real, albeit limited, field for practical application.

DS may have been the most influential single current in the PT in Porto Alegre, but it did not have things all its own way. It never had an automatic majority of its own. The right wing of the PT was not strong in Porto Alegre, but DS did have to share the terrain with several other currents on the left and a number of centrist groupings, like the group around Tarso Genro. They all had somewhat different approaches to participatory democracy. Even within DS, there was not monolithic agreement on every detail.

DIFFERENCES OVER THE PT WAY OF GOVERNING

It was this particular cocktail of ingredients, both inside the PT and in the wider social movement, that blended to create the participatory budget in Porto Alegre and led to the city becoming the benchmark for the 'PT way of governing'.

Most people defined the 'PT way of governing' through much of the 1990s as a simple combination: inversion of social priorities plus popular participation. All wings of the party generally accepted this dual characterisation. Implicitly it put the practice of participatory budgets – pioneered in Porto Alegre – at the centre of the PT's project for local government, and eventually for national government as well. The two achievements claimed for the PB were in fact that it inverted spending priorities in favour of the poorest neighbourhoods and that it promoted active participation by the population in managing public affairs.

The formula was ambiguous from the beginning, however. Most party leaders did not share the DS interpretation. Even in Porto Alegre it co-existed with more moderate interpretations.[10] Beyond Porto Alegre, in most other cities where PT administrations implemented participatory budgets, these more moderate interpretations were even more explicit. In a whole series of other non-PT local governments, in Brazil and abroad, the distance from the DS interpretation was greater still. Assis Brasil, in charge of the Porto Alegre city hall's department for Community Relations Coordination, put it like this:

> We have to ask ourselves what participatory budget we're talking about. Because just as there are various sorts of socialism, so today even the World Bank can recommend the participatory budget. But is that the participatory budget we want? The Radical Civic Union, which elected Fernando de la Rua president in Argentina,[11] paid us various visits to study the PB and said it was in favour of doing the same. The French Socialist Party was here at the World Social Forum and said it was in favour of implementing the participatory budget in France. But the reason the World Bank is in favour of the PB is that it likes the transparency it provides. As a funding body it wants to know that its money is being used for the purposes agreed and not being siphoned off into somebody's pocket.
>
> This debate has never been had out in the PT. Why? Because there are sectors of the PT who think that really is what the PB is for: greater transparency, more efficient investments and a little bit of social justice thrown in for good measure. They don't go any further than that. There are other sectors that put more emphasis on promoting social justice and a strong sense of citizenship. That's certainly important, but the PB has to be more than that. For example, Santo Andre, one of the industrial suburbs of São Paulo, has a participatory budget. But there, unlike Porto Alegre, half the members of the PB Council come from the government side, and only half from the population. And there the government members have the right to vote too. That's a very clear limitation on establishing a more advanced form of democracy. Our tradition, on the other hand, points to the PB as an element of rupture, as a step towards another kind of state, another way of running society, which is our programmatic vision of a self-managed socialism. I'm not saying that's what exists at the moment. But there are elements pointing in that direction.
>
> So I think this is the debate we now need, about where the PB is leading. Because the discussion about what kind of socialism we on the left want to build passes through this debate about where the PB is headed.

NEOLIBERALISM WITHIN THE PT

Towards the end of the 1990s, however, it became increasingly clear that even the existing room for ambiguity in the 'PT way of governing' was not enough for some core sections of the PT leadership. The example of Santo Andre, and its mayor at the time, Celso Daniel, is a good illustration.

Daniel first became mayor of this key industrial suburb of São Paulo in 1989, in the first wave of PT local governments that included Porto Alegre. He served a second term from 1997 to 2000 and had begun a third when he was kidnapped and murdered late in 2001 in circumstances that remain unclear.[12] The PB process he helped to introduce in his time in office was, at first sight, a carbon copy of the Porto Alegre experience. However, there were some significant differences. Organisationally, as Assis Brasil points out, half the PB council in Santo Andre consisted of representatives of city hall, nominated by the mayor and with the right to vote. Indeed, a two-thirds-majority rule on the PB presiding committee gave the local government representatives an effective veto in case of major disagreements.

Behind these apparently minor constitutional differences lay a distinct philosophy. The Santo Andre version of the PB never envisaged a wholesale transfer of sovereign power to the people, of the kind that Raul Pont argues for elsewhere in this book. It always saw the PB rather as a form of 'dialogue', of 'powersharing' between city hall and civil society. Its aim was to 'involve' the population in the business of local government, not to hand control over to them.

Daniel's importance went well beyond Santo Andre. Lula and other PT leaders regarded him highly as both an administrator and an intellectual, and gave him responsibility for coordinating the drawing up of the PT's governmental programme ahead of the 2002 presidential election campaign. In this capacity, Daniel was at the centre of the PT's political evolution in this critical period. Had he lived, he would probably have taken charge of organising the handover to the PT government and then assumed a key post in Lula's cabinet, possibly as finance minister. In the event both these tasks passed to Antonio Palocci, the PT mayor of Ribeirão Preto, another city in São Paulo state, who had been moving even faster in the direction of market-led economic priorities.

Three years before Lula's election, in 1999, Daniel wrote the keynote contribution to a collection of essays called *Governo e Cidadania* ('Governance and Citizenship') on 'the PT way of governing' published by the PT's own publishing house.[13] Entitled 'Local Management on the Threshold of a New Millennium', Daniel's article is a fascinating foretaste of the direction in which the PT's leaders and policymakers were heading.

On the one hand it reasserts, in terms very similar to the Governmental Programme Guidelines adopted at the PT's National Conference in December 2001, the party's longstanding commitment to a break with the neoliberal economic model – or to a 'battle of ideas with the neoliberal litany'. On the other hand, it devotes most of its energies to arguing that the traditional view of the PT way of governing – combining the inversion of social priorities with popular participation – is no longer sufficient. While claiming to retain both, it seeks to relocate them in the context of 'a new relation between public and private'.

Concretely this means, for example, no longer just concentrating on correcting the huge imbalance in urban infrastructure by improving basic services (water, sewage, paving) in the slum areas generally known in Brazil as 'the periphery'. PT administrations should increasingly combine investments in peripheral neighbourhoods with big development projects in 'the city centre', which can improve the quality of life for all the city's inhabitants, Daniel suggests, and with income and job-creation programmes that promote economic development for the whole city. The false opposition between centre and periphery must be overcome, he argues.

This may not seem like a significant departure. But the drift becomes clearer when Daniel moves on to argue that the other half of the legacy from PT administrations in the early 1990s – the emphasis on popular participation – now needs urgently to be supplemented with a new agenda of 'administrative modernisation'. This, he soon makes clear, means slimming down local government. Expenditure on local government employees' wages and pensions may well have to be cut in order to preserve the capacity for investment that is at the heart of the participatory budget. At the same time mechanisms of collective participation and control like the participatory budget need to be supplemented with mechanisms of 'individual' participation and control. Daniel proposes a modern system of reporting on targets and delivery, open to individual citizen scrutiny and redress through an ombudsman.

Moreover, Daniel says, there is no particular reason why so many local services should remain in the hands of the local state. Education and health may be fair enough, but transport for example can surely be handed over to the private sector. The important thing in this new vision he was developing just before he was killed is that there should be public control, or perhaps just public supervision, over provision of public services, whether the provider is public or private.

EXTREME AMBIGUITY

This new formulation pushes the old ambiguity in the PT's debates to new extremes. The idea of public (or popular) control over parts of the private sector can, of course, be interpreted in a very radical sense. In traditional Marxist theory, the concept of workers' control has this meaning. In João Machado's contribution at the end of this book, he develops the idea of an 'economy of cooperation and solidarity' in a similar direction, pointing to the production cooperatives set up by the Landless Workers' Movement (MST) for example as a counterpart in the economic sphere to the participatory budget in the political sphere.

But it is much easier to read Celso Daniel's use of these formulations as a lurch to the right, with strong echoes of Tony Blair's 'third way' defence of the free market as a social market. We seem to be seeing the beginnings of a move to import some key neoliberal tenets into the heart of the PT project.

The fact that by the first years of the twenty-first century such very different political propositions could still be expressed in the same language within the PT, and still take the participatory budget as a point of reference, may help explain the huge tensions and widely divergent interpretations that accompanied the first year or more of Lula's presidency after January 2003.

The same extreme ambiguity helps explain how some others on the left have been able to dismiss Porto Alegre's participatory budget as an elaborate confidence trick. João Penha for example argues that the PB is little short of a World Bank-inspired plot to involve the poor in cutting their own wages and services.[14] As such, he sees it as essentially another mechanism to ensure the surplus needed to keep up payments on Brazil's foreign debt. The texts in the rest of this book should make clear how difficult it is to recognise either the theory or the practice of Porto Alegre's PB in Penha's description. But at the other end of the ambiguity, there *may be* areas of the PT's theory and practice, including some versions of the PB, that come closer to matching his account.

DEBATES IN THE GLOBAL JUSTICE MOVEMENT

There are at least two ways in which this debate over the PB relates to wider ambiguities facing the left and the movement for a different kind of globalisation. First, the challenges facing the new Brazilian government in 2003 were clearly a practical expression of the challenges that the global movement had been debating and publicising ever since Seattle: what to do about debt, free trade, genetically modified organisms (GMOs), food security and all the other familiar problems. Lula's ability or failure to break with the neoliberal model, and his recourse to or renunciation of instruments of participatory democracy as means to achieve this break – along the lines suggested by Raul Pont above – would be not only a test for the PT in Brazil. They would be also a test for the entire international movement of World Social Forums that had chosen to make Porto Alegre its symbolic capital.[15]

This in turn exposes a whole set of conceptual and strategic ambiguities that have long characterised the global justice movement *and* which characterise the participatory budget process as well. In one sense these ambiguities have been a part of the movement's strength, a condition of its breadth and diversity. But the experience of the Lula government suggests they may also be a source of great vulnerability. As we suggested at the outset, these ambiguities go back way before Seattle. The experience of at least the first part of the PT's period in government in Brasilia shows that addressing them is now an urgent task for the movement as a whole.

Take a cluster of concepts that comes up around the participatory budget: 'community', 'participation', 'empowerment'. There are others, like 'horizontal', 'dialogue' and 'decentralise'. Their history over the last few decades helps us to understand how the participatory budget has managed to have such a wide appeal.

By the 1970s and early 1980s these terms had become common currency on the left, especially among non-governmental organisations and social movements in North and South. Often they were used as semi-synonymous with traditional Marxist concepts, like 'class', 'workers' control', 'emancipation' or 'proletarian democracy'. In the North, in situations of tight ideological constraint, the language of 'community' was less embarrassing. In Latin America and other areas of widespread torture and disappearances, it was just plain safer.

Much of this language originated with Brazilian educationalist Paulo Freire and others influenced by him.[16] The theory and practice of horizontal organisation and communication that Freire and his followers developed overlapped with the language of liberation theology, which had its own philosophical reasons for not adopting directly the vocabulary of Marxist orthodoxy. Through the movement of grassroots church communities, their legacy figured largely in the formation of the PT and in the dense network of neighbourhood organisations in Porto Alegre – the two forces that gave birth to the participatory budget in 1989.

But 1989 also saw the crystallisation of a parallel process – one of several conceptual counterparts to the collapse of the Soviet bloc. The long decay of Stalinist politics had been accelerating for a number of years. Post-Althusserian Marxism had been transmuting into postmodernism. En route, it encountered a variety of liberal and even right-wing libertarian currents heading in the opposite direction. As the Wall came down, themes like community, decentralisation and participation provided them with a set of common leitmotifs.

In much of Latin America, institutions like the Ford Foundation and World Bank began pouring money into projects to strengthen local democracy and civil society, many of them run by former revolutionaries. In Northern universities, postmodernists savaged theories of Third World 'dependency' – developed most famously by leading Brazilian Marxist sociologist Fernando Henrique Cardoso (a couple of decades before he became the country's most consistently neoliberal president). The word 'imperialism' had long become taboo. To cite just one example, the prestigious Institute of Development Studies at Sussex University in southern England, with close links to the new third-way thinking about development issues in several European capitals, became entranced with the theory of 'Participatory Rural Appraisal'.[17] This 'paradigm shift' combined an apparently radical extension of democratic participation at the local level, in this case Third World rural communities, with an apparently uncritical acceptance of the existing macroeconomic framework. In a whole variety of academic and policy areas, the vocabulary of emancipation was now being deployed to justify the neoliberal rollback of the state.

A NEW LANGUAGE OF LIBERATION

These two, diametrically opposed uses of the vocabulary of participation may correspond, very approximately, to the two conflicting visions of the participatory budget.

The latter part of the 1990s brought a third element into the picture. The rise of the worldwide movement for global justice brought with it the emergence of a new, radical, libertarian strand making its own use of some of the same 'horizontal' concepts. Whatever its merits or shortcomings, this libertarian strand of activism did more to revive the ideas and confidence of the left than any other political movement for a generation or more.

The starting point was of course the 1994 Zapatista uprising in Chiapas. The Zapatistas insisted that they did not want to seize power but merely help to open up the spaces within which others could build their own power. The variations on this theme since then have been almost endless: the rebirth of old-fashioned anarchism and the emergence of a new autonomism in Europe, Hardt and Negri's 'multitude', the greater visibility of indigenous movements and other expressions of 'identity' politics in much of Latin America and other parts of the South.

The international nature of the movement has revealed the international extent of these shifts. In India, for example, as Mumbai took over, temporarily, from Porto Alegre as the new venue for the World Social Forum, the centre of attention seemed to have moved from an earlier cycle of local democracy – symbolised by the Communist Party-led and -inspired experience in Kerala – to a new cycle of 'localisation', as represented by the Jaiv Panchayats or Living Democracy movement in Uttaranchal. Here traditional forms of village government have been reinvented and democratised in an effort to protect local biodiversity from international patents, GM seeds and export-led monoculture.[18]

Closer to home, and of more immediate relevance for the participatory budget in Porto Alegre is the experience in Argentina since the uprising that overthrew Fernando de la Rua in December 2001. For many on the new libertarian left, as well as for many more orthodox Marxists, the extraordinary breadth and intensity of self-organisation that emerged in those months looked much more like the kind of independent, direct democracy they were espousing than the PB in Porto Alegre, with its half-in, half-out relationship to the existing state. Some explicitly counterposed the two. However, the spectacular inability of anyone on the left to build on the spontaneous outburst in Argentina and produce any lasting political outcome has led to fresh soulsearching among the most sensitive representatives of both the libertarian and orthodox camps.[19]

A fuller discussion of these issues would go far beyond the scope of this book. But they deserve attention. The stakes are both theoretical and practical. What exactly are the similarities and differences between the experiences of direct democracy represented by the participatory budget in Porto Alegre, the popular assemblies in Buenos Aires, and the autonomous, Zapatista municipalities in Chiapas?

Re-examined in this light, the PB appears to sit at the intersection of these different strands. In its radical, Porto Alegre variant, it may have something to say to both the libertarian and orthodox traditions about the problem of the state and how a credible alternative can be established. It may even hold out a possibility of synthesis between traditional Marxist aims and the neo-Zapatista thinking that holds sway in much of the global justice movement. But it is also clear, as João Machado argues in the final chapter of this book, that without constantly engaging with these strategic issues the PB runs a constant risk of being coopted by the neoliberal variant of participatory democracy.

2
From First Steps
to Final Strategies

Iain Bruce

The people directly involved in Porto Alegre's participatory budget never tire of telling you that it is an open-ended process – a kind of work in progress. If we take a closer look, through their eyes, at how that process has evolved since 1989, then we should also get a clearer idea of where it is now, and where they think it might be heading in the future. The account that follows is taken from a series of extended interviews with some of the PB's key architects and practitioners in the city of Porto Alegre and the state of Rio Grande do Sul. Ubiratan de Souza, André Passos Cordeiro and Raul Pont have all contributed their own chapters to this book. Assis Brasil Olegario Filho, already introduced in the previous chapter, has worked closely with the others since the very earliest days of the participatory budget.[1] Their story begins at the beginning.

ORIGINS

When the PT campaigned for Porto Alegre's mayoral elections in the southern spring of 1988, there was no mention of the participatory budget in its programme. What was widely agreed within the party was the aim of governing with popular councils. Raul Pont recalls,

> We didn't have much idea what they might be. It was very theoretical, because we had no real experience of anything like that in Brazil. But we did say in our programme that we wanted to govern with the population, with the participation of the people, through popular councils.

This reflected of course the Marxist background of many of those involved. The point of reference, for both these PT members and their electoral allies in the old Brazilian Communist Party (PCB), were the Paris Commune and the workers' councils or soviets of the early years of the Russian Revolution. Their aim was to translate these general elements of a socialist programme into their own local reality.

Indeed there was no prior experience anywhere in Brazil of anything resembling the participatory budget that began to emerge in Porto Alegre in 1989 and 1990. More than a decade earlier, during the years of military dictatorship, Pont had helped to form a Socialist Tendency inside the only legal opposition party, the Brazilian Democratic Movement (MDB). He remembers that one or two local governments run by the MDB in other parts of Brazil had begun to experiment with forms of participation, bringing together the population to hear what they had to say. 'Under a military dictatorship, that was obviously an advance. But it was insufficient.'

What did already exist in Porto Alegre was a dense history of community organisation through neighbourhood associations. In some regions of the city like Glória, which we came across in the Prologue, these neighbourhood organisations were already meeting together to share experiences and combine struggles in what they themselves called 'popular councils'. This community movement had played a significant part in the struggle against the military dictatorship in the 1970s and for direct elections in 1983 and 1984. This led in the mid 1980s to the creation of the Union of Neighbourhood Associations of Porto Alegre (UAMPA), which brought together most of these organisations. UAMPA had a clear left leadership linked to the PT, but included members and sympathisers of other left parties and people from the old populist tradition.[2]

One of the most important struggles that shaped the community movement in the late 1980s was the struggle over public transport, demanding better service and lower fares. Together with struggles for housing and basic sanitation, the transport struggle consolidated the community movement as an autonomous expression of the city's poorest sections. The populist mayor at the time[3] tried to introduce a law that would have tied the popular councils born from the struggles to local government. So there was already an experience of fighting to defend the movement's autonomy.

Another factor that fed into the emergence of the movement was the big wave of migration from the countryside to the city at the end of the 1970s and throughout the 1980s. The migration resulted in ever-bigger concentrations of population, entirely lacking in services, on the edges of Porto Alegre. There was no adequate urban infrastructure, no health facilities and no schools. During the military dictatorship, the regime nominated mayors of state capitals, so the only way to obtain public services was to mobilise for them in the streets. Ubiratan de Souza remembers the community movement at that time having to build barricades across the streets to demand that they be properly paved.

When the PT and its Popular Front allies elected Olívio Dutra mayor in the 1988 elections, the community movement expected immediate results. After all, this was a government of the left, so they assumed that the demands they had been making for the previous 20 years for decent public services on the periphery of Porto Alegre would be met. But there was an early impasse. The outgoing local government, which had been squeezing down wages throughout its mandate, suddenly gave the council workforce a 110 per cent pay rise in its very last month in office in December 1988. This committed 98 per cent of the council's current account budget for the following year to wage costs. The lame duck administration also granted an amnesty to all those who had arrears on their council buildings tax, or IPTU, which is the most important local source of revenue for municipal governments in Brazil. There were long queues of people waiting to pay off their arrears at a specially reduced rate.

This made it very difficult for the incoming PT administration to sustain, let alone increase, its revenue. With the community movement pressing at the same time for more services in the poorest areas, Dutra's new local government decided to open up the council budget to public scrutiny. It wanted to show why it was impossible to make investments in new services given the council's existing level of income and the commitments already made.

The current coordinator of the PB in Porto Alegre, André Passos, was still in his teens at the time, but already an active member of the PT. He says that this peculiar mixture of circumstances is where it all began. The financial difficulties facing the new administration, combined with its commitment to work with a well-organised population, the existence of neighbourhood associations grouped in popular councils, the huge expectations of the population in general and some rather generic references to the socialist programme produced a situation of some tension, which forced the government to come up with some way of making itself accountable. That was the beginning of the participatory budget.

FIRST STEPS

There were plenty of problems to overcome just to get started. The traditions of Brazilian populism still heavily influenced much of the community movement. Practices of patronage and paternalism – local politicians trading votes for promises of special treatment for particular neighbourhoods – were rife. On the other hand, the local administration's planning structure, which divided the city into four regions, central, north, east, and south (Guaiba Lake lies to Porto Alegre's west), was very bureaucratic and undemocratic. Technocrats dominated the process completely; popular participation was minimal.

The participatory budget began as a proposal for an annual discussion of the municipal budget on the basis of these four regions. 'The question was, what exactly would the popular councils discuss?' As Raul Pont recalls, their options were limited.

Since there were no resources, up until the middle of the second year the only thing we could really discuss was improving delivery of some services. Rubbish collection for example. There were some favelas or slum areas that didn't have even the most rudimentary rubbish collection. They'd been simply abandoned by previous administrations. Others had almost no street lighting. The town hall already had workers and equipment in those areas, so it was relatively easy to improve and extend those services. But investment as such only began in the second year with the tax reform.

Municipal governments in Brazil have long been heavily dependent on the money that federal and state governments return to them.

However, Brazil's 1988 constitution – the first after military rule – and the Rio Grande do Sul state constitution the following year did give municipalities more scope to raise their own taxes as well as a bigger share of national taxes. As a result, the municipalities' share of total tax revenue rose from 11–12 per cent to 16–17 per cent. Mayor Dutra's first PT administration took advantage of this shift to introduce a series of tax reforms of its own. The most important reform modified the basic buildings tax, or IPTU. It replaced the single existing tax band with a much wider, progressive scale based on the simple principle that those who had more should pay more.

At the same time, as a way of combating the structures of paternalism and populism, the administration proposed to the community the principle of direct participation. That meant one person, one vote. Nobody represented anyone else, nobody got to vote two or three times as president of an association, and nobody was delegated from a community group or trade union or anything of that sort.

One of the first things people demanded that first year was greater decentralisation. The community movement proposed the existing four regions be split up into a total of 16, to make discussions more democratic and relevant and allow more people to take part. That first budget for the year 1990 concentrated the very limited resources available in the four poorest regions. In the meantime the community movement and PT administration organised *'mutiroes'* – weekends of voluntary work – when people came together to help clean up a particular neighbourhood.

After 1990, as a result of higher revenue due mainly to reform of the IPTU and a clampdown on tax evasion, it became possible to decide on investments and services for all 16 regions. In the process, agreement was reached on three basic criteria for how these resources should be distributed among the regions, which have been in effect ever since: (1) priorities adopted by the PB in that region; (2) the extent to which basic infrastructure and services are lacking in that region; and (3) the size of the population served.

According to Raul Pont, when people began to see the fruits of these budget discussions in terms of real results on the ground, real investments in real paving on their streets, support for the participatory budget began to spread like wildfire.

ACHIEVEMENTS AND OBSTACLES

Porto Alegre is not an island

Before talking about the participatory budget's achievements, we need to recall what community leader José Brizola said in the Prologue: Porto Alegre is not an island. It never escaped the Brazilian reality of the 1990s and early 2000s. The overarching feature of these years was the impact of neoliberal globalisation and spiralling foreign debt, and the accompanying policies of privatisation and deregulation implemented by successive governments in Brasilia guided by the multilateral financial institutions in Washington.

The figures speak for themselves. Brazil has long been one of the most unequal countries on the planet. Different studies, using slightly different criteria, place it second, third or fourth in the world league of income disparities, somewhere behind Sierra Leone and possibly Paraguay. Porto Alegre and the state of Rio Grande do Sul may be relatively more affluent than much of the country; but a study by the municipal government shows that between 1981–85 and 1995–99 inequality in the Porto Alegre Metropolitan Region rose by 16.4 per cent. Unemployment increased over the same period by 78.4 per cent. Child labour (of 10–14-year-olds) increased by 11 per cent. The proportion of the population classified as poor increased by 19.8 per cent. Overall the poverty index went up by 100 per cent.[4] As in other major Brazilian cities, urban violence, often linked to the drug trade, reached unprecedented levels.

One factor feeding into these indices of rising unemployment, poverty and violence was the federal government's withdrawal from many of its already minimal social commitments. During the third PT administration in Porto Alegre (1997–2000), with Pont as mayor, the central government eliminated its spending on inexpensive housing programmes across Brazil. In the same year, 1998, the central government cut its spending on sanitation to less than a quarter of the previous level – and tied up most of what was left in financing privatisation of water and sewage services. Federal bodies dealing with social services were abolished.

At the same time that local governments had to take over many responsibilities abandoned by Brasilia, the federal government introduced a series of measures that once again reduced the municipalities' share of national tax income. From a high point of about 18 per cent, the localities' share fell back to around 14 per cent.

It is against this background that the achievements of the PT administration in Porto Alegre and the participatory budget have to be judged. These achievements can be divided into three: concrete social improvements, levels of popular mobilisation, and the extent to which a new political relationship with the state has been established.

Turning around social priorities

Simply in terms of practical reforms, these achievements have been significant. It is no accident that the PB in Porto Alegre became the benchmark for both pillars of the 'PT way of governing'; that is, not only extending popular participation but also radically turning around local government's social priorities.

We have already seen how in its first year, faced with a complete dearth of resources, the PB chose to concentrate all its efforts in the poorest neighbourhoods. In the budget for 1991, the five regions classified as 'most in need' received 70 per cent of the resources. The other eleven got 30 per cent. The following year this principle – 'to each according to their need' – was incorporated into the set of criteria laid out in the rulebook adopted through the PB process itself. (See Part II – How it Works.)

Those involved in the PB call the outcome a 'virtuous circle'. Since the most deprived parts of the population have turned out in the largest numbers to take part in PB debates and vote, naturally enough their neighbourhoods have gained the bulk of new investment in works and services. Obviously this coincides with the PT administration's own priorities, but the main impulse has come from outside city hall. Once the ball was set rolling, it acquired its own momentum. André Passos and Raul Pont cite some of the results later in this book: 99.5 per cent of the population now connected to the water mains and 83 per cent to the sewage system; big increases in the number of creches and of streets that have been paved.

Given the overall context of a continuing neoliberal offensive that has sharpened inequalities and deepened poverty throughout Brazil, these figures are impressive enough. But, for the contributors to this book, it is less the numbers that are important than the logic.

Take public transport. Flying in the face of pressures to privatise public services, Porto Alegre has built up what is generally considered the best bus service in Brazil, centred on a publicly owned bus company. This has been achieved through a variety of participatory mechanisms, including a citywide transport forum, one of the six 'thematic plenaries' added to the PB system after 1984 to take better account of needs that cut across several communities. But regional PB discussions have also played a part. By demanding paved streets and other improvements in local access, the local assemblies helped change the logic governing public transport in Porto Alegre. The system was designed first and foremost – as in most parts of the world – to meet the needs of capital. Bus routes were drawn up primarily with a view to funneling the workforce in and out of the city centre. Now improved access makes a network of routes possible that serves the needs and expressed wishes of the poorest neighbourhoods. Buses reach further into poor neighbourhoods and make cross-city links so that people in one poor area can travel directly to visit friends or family in another poor area.

Another example is the legalisation of the city's many urban squats. Against the initial advice of local government experts, communities have used a loophole in the federal constitution to win the most advanced local legislation in the country on this question. This in turn has helped them get funds for sanitation, water and electricity connections, and other basic services.

A mobilised population

A continuing series of reformulations to the rules, debated and decided by the participants themselves, have encouraged more people to participate and made the PB more responsive to their needs. From just 900 people in the PB's first year in Porto Alegre, the number taking part increased to 5,000 or 6,000 in 1992, when the first fruits of the first investments were becoming apparent. The fact that people continued to see real results, and could demand explanations if they did not, fed further mobilisations. The numbers continued to climb past the 15,000 mark when the 'thematic plenaries' were added to the process in 1994, and reached upwards of 30,000 in the early 2000s.

Admittedly some pre-existing social movements, neighbourhood associations and trade unions feared that the PB would circumvent and weaken their own organisations. Assis Brasil, currently in charge of the body that coordinates relations between city hall and the community, recalls the case of the Communist Party of Brazil:

> The comrades from the PCdoB, and even some from the PT too, thought the president of a neighbourhood association should automatically be its delegate. No, but he's been the president for 20 years, they'd say. Or she's been the treasurer for 15 years. You're trying to undermine the popular organisations. This kind of attitude still exists, but now it's in a very small minority.

Activists did not only try to defend existing spheres of influence, but were also genuinely afraid that the principle of universal participation and direct democracy would atomise the community movement into isolated individuals. If anything, the PB has had the opposite effect. On the one hand, deciding things by direct vote has encouraged ordinary citizens, who have never been members of any party or social organisation, to become involved. On the other hand, it has also provided an arena and an incentive for community organisations to mobilise their members, so that they too attend PB assemblies and vote for their priorities.

As a result, Assis Brasil points out, the number of such community organisations has grown spectacularly. Moreover their distribution has evened out. They used to be concentrated in four or five well-organised areas like Gloria, while in other areas like Cristal or the centre there was almost nothing. Now the most active organisations have won new legitimacy, and many new ones have sprung up.

The only organisations that have lost out are phantom movements and associations that proved unable to mobilise the people they claim to represent, including community organisations that were essentially fronts or relays for an array of right-wing parties and local politicians.

The last few years have however seen the number of people participating in the PB flatten out. The city hall's own figures indicate that there was even a slight dip in 2002. This may be an accounting problem; 2002 was the year that the PB in Porto Alegre followed the example of the PB at state level and replaced the two rounds of regional assemblies (where the number of participants is strictly recorded) with a single round. Much of the discussion took place instead at preparatory meetings at neighbourhood and street level, where no register of numbers is kept. But it may also point to one of the strategic problems raised by Sérgio Baierle[5] and others. How long can the PB keep developing without either hitting a ceiling or breaking through the local and national structures that contain it? Put more bluntly, has the PB run out of steam, and if so, is this unavoidable?

A new relation with the state

The answers to these questions depend in part how we judge the other area of achievement claimed for the PB: its ability, through the kind of mobilisation described above, to produce a new relationship between the people and the state.

The contributors to this book argue that the PB has shown tens of thousands of working and poor people that there is an alternative to the passive, increasingly disillusioned delegation of power that characterises the prevailing systems of representative democracy. The PB has shown them that they can take at least some of this power back into their own hands. As such it points towards another kind of democracy, which bears a striking resemblance to the kind of socialist democracy many in the PT had long been dreaming of.

Pont points out that while some PT activists and leaders with a background in Marxist politics may have had at least an abstract, historical acquaintance with experiences of self-management, workers' councils and the like, the bulk of the population had no knowledge of any of this. Nonetheless, participants in the PB have worked out a profound critique of representative democracy and pointed towards the need to go beyond it in practice.

The limitations of the representative system, Pont says, became particularly obvious in Brazil. In Brazil, unlike most European countries, the separation of powers between legislature and executive is total. The executive – the president at federal level, the governor at state level and the mayor at municipal level – has virtually the power of an emperor within his or her own domain. This means that a public budget in Brazil, both nationally and locally, has merely *authorising* status. Budgets tell mayors or presidents what they *can* spend, if they feel like it. It does not tell them what they *must* spend. Indeed the so-called 'programme budget', which lets the population know how much they can expect to be spent on what and lets them demand an explanation if it is not, never existed in Brazil until the participatory budget introduced it. So as Pont says,

> for the mayor of Porto Alegre, at the beginning of the 1990s, to give up his control over the budget and hand over to the population the power to decide directly all the new works and services that should be funded, meant an absolute subversion of the representative system, especially in its Brazilian form.

For Pont, the history of the traditional representative system is inseparable from the history of capitalism; the former has developed as a means for sustaining the latter. 'In so far as we are developing a system where that sovereignty is shifted from the executive to direct participation by the people, we are creating the basis, generating the awareness and political education, that are needed for change.' How far this can go is difficult to predict, he says; it will depend in part on whether those in the PT who share this vision are able to win the strategic debate in the party.

The PT in Porto Alegre, where the experience is most developed, has a special responsibility to carry on the debate and develop the theory. This work is still in its infancy. Academics, the various left currents and those directly involved need to do much more to develop a practical, radical critique of the representative system. This does not mean denying the importance of democracy, but rather insisting on the need to deepen and radicalise it, on the need for *more* democracy, with more popular control and less delegation of power. The PB is only one element here. It must be combined with other instruments: municipal councils; sectoral councils dealing with health and education, which already have a certain tradition in Brazil; and the regular use of referendums. Previous examples in Europe and elsewhere of self-management and workers' control of production must also be studied, in order to understand how they might relate to popular participation in the political sphere. Pont says,

> We have a big challenge here dealing with experiences of non-state, public control. Even the left in the PT is resistant to these ideas, because many people have that bureaucratic, Stalinist conception, that either the state controls everything and everyone is a public employee, or else it's capitalism. I think that's wrong. If we do not have the audacity to think through such forms of public control, then we will end up with states that may be more democratic in important ways, but which will end up generating their own forms of bureaucracy.

Nonetheless, some of the PB's positive lessons are already clear. It points towards a new kind of executive and a new kind of legislature. It shows in practice that it is possible to combat the bureaucratisation and corruption that exist in the representative state. It opens the way towards a more direct form of democracy.

What are the limits of direct democracy? Does Pont think we are talking here about Rousseau's utopia, where there is *no* delegation, *no* transfer of power, and sovereignty remains completely undivided? 'Well I think the closer we can get to that, the better', he says. But for the time being he is more interested in pushing the process forward than in worrying about where its limits lie.

Limits of local action

Long before the participatory budget reaches its theoretical limits in a city like Porto Alegre, unfortunately, it runs up against some more concrete constraints. One of the central principles of this form of public control, as Ubiratan de Souza explains later in Chapter 3 of this book, is that the PB should have control over the *whole* of the budget, not just a part of it. This itself is an expression of the principle that sovereignty is indivisible.

The first problem, however, is that a city government like Porto Alegre's has a limited jurisdiction. For example, there is no point in the people of Gloria voting for the municipal budget to be spent on putting more police officers on the street to combat the drug-related violence that afflicts many of their poorest neighbourhoods. The Brazilian statutory framework gives municipal governments almost no powers over policing. That falls under the state governments.

Parallel constraints appear within the area that does fall under municipal responsibility. For example, the Porto Alegre-style PB *does* have the right, in principle, to decide upon and alter the whole of the municipal budget. The PB rulebook explicitly grants this power to the PB council, made up of delegates from the public assemblies (see the fuller description of PB mechanisms in Part II). As such this is way ahead of the more limited forms of PB practised by some more moderate PT administrations elsewhere in Brazil.

However, in practice the whole of the budget is not discussed, especially not by the population as a whole. What the open public assemblies actually debate and decide are the priorities for new capital works and a limited number of related services. The investment component of this, which is the bulk of it, corresponded in 2003 to just 12.28 per cent of the total direct municipal budget. Some of the reasons for this 'self-limitation' are fairly straightforward. Much of the budget is tied up in paying the municipal workforce's wages. Wages in turn depend on collective agreements with public service unions, which left-wing administrations are obviously committed to honouring. Other costs are also comparatively rigid. The municipal electricity and phone bills cannot be dramatically changed from year to year, nor can the local government decide not to do any street cleaning. Federal and municipal statutes also oblige the city hall to spend at least 30 per cent of its budget on education and at least 13 per cent on health. (In fact in 2003 Porto Alegre allocated 31 per cent to education and 19 per cent to health.)

But other factors also come into play. They relate to another of the areas questioned by Sérgio Baierle: the difficulty the Porto Alegre PB has had in giving the mobilised population a really effective role in formulating policy. Assis Brasil puts it like this:

There's a part of local government where we've made little progress in terms of establishing popular control. In addition to investments, we do have such control over some services, like the community creches, the family assistance programme, which is a kind of minimum basic income, and the decentralisation of cultural activities. But there's a real lack when it comes to the main service areas, provided by the works department, the drainage department, water service and so forth. The PB council does vote on general allocations to these areas in the overall budget. But there's no discussion of the detail of what's spent where or what the policy criteria should be.

The problem here is the balance of forces within the PT and at city hall, because this would interfere with some established centres of power in local government. It would raise uncomfortable questions about the role of departmental secretaries and so forth. This is something we've begun to discuss in a decentralisation working group involving my own department, the community relations council, André's planning cabinet, and the secretaries of planning, finance and administration. It was also a central discussion at the Fourth City Congress, concluded in June 2003, which was called to discuss the achievements and limitations of participatory democracy in Porto Alegre. But we still have a long way to go.

Last but not least, the total funds available for municipal spending are woefully inadequate and strictly controlled. The details are complicated, but as mentioned before only 14 per cent of total tax revenue in Brazil is available to municipal administrations. Most of it is handed back to city halls by federal and state governments, making control from the centre even stronger. The participatory budget did help the PT administration in Porto Alegre to increase its room for manoeuvre, first by cracking down on the endemic corruption of previous local governments, and second by backing moves for more progressive taxation, especially on real estate. Locally raised taxation went up by 196 per cent in the first ten years of the PT administration. But the net result is that the PB's real sovereignty over public spending in Porto Alegre remains severely curtailed.

STRATEGIC CHOICES

There are two or three ways of looking at these limitations. Broadly speaking, they correspond to the different strategic approaches to 'the PT way of governing' outlined in Chapter 1.

For the neoliberal right and the social-democratic centre, the limitations are not really a problem. They simply confirm that participatory democracy cannot change the system, only ameliorate its operations and impact. We can call this the conservative, compensatory approach to participatory democracy. A curiously similar line of reasoning leads some on the far left to conclude that the PB is just another variant of reformism, trapped in the logic of the capitalist state.

Those who adopt the third approach – represented with a variety of emphases in the contributions that make up the rest of this book – see these limitations as both a major obstacle and a major opportunity. They are part of what de Souza calls the continual process of contradiction, rupture and synthesis that characterises the participatory budget.

From this point of view, it is crucial to understand how the PB combines its two kinds of achievement. First, it mobilises the population to bring about practical improvements in their local environment. But second, in so far as this mobilisation *begins* to exert power over parts of the local state, it is also a process of political education. Not only are the opaque mechanisms of public finances demystified for thousands of ordinary working-class citizens, important as that certainly is. These citizens also become aware very quickly of the *limitations* of this kind of local action. They can see for themselves how the Brazilian statutory framework imposes very tight restrictions on what a city hall administration can do.

This is what Assis Brasil means by the ambiguous nature of the participatory budget. On the one hand it is a partnership, a system of co-management, between city hall and the population within the local capitalist state. On the other hand, he says, 'it is an embryonic form of dual power'. That is, the PB can also be seen as the beginnings of a new set of political institutions, which could ultimately become the basis for an alternative form of state power. This, he adds, has some very obvious limitations.

> Of course it's limited to the context of one municipality, or one state, in a country like Brazil. The objective and subjective circumstances make it impossible to call here and now, as some to the PT's left do, for 'All Power to the Participatory Budget'.[6] But it does have this aspect to it, and that's something we have to push as far as we can.

This brings us back to where we started: the contradiction at the heart of the PB.

THE CENTRAL CONTRADICTION

To sum up, all the achievements of the participatory budget – the real reforms, the mobilisation, increased political awareness, the whole new relationship with the state – run up against the straightjacket of the existing legal, constitutional and fiscal framework. This in turn underpins the neoliberal macroeconomic policies of successive governments in Brasilia, including those adopted so zealously at the beginning of the Lula administration.

This central contradiction can go in any one of three directions. It could simply be cut short by electoral defeat. This is a real possibility, and it might or might not be a consequence of the PB's own inadequacies. In his last contribution to Part III of this book, Pont insists that the PT's defeat in the Rio Grande do Sul state elections in October 2002 was *not* a reflection on the PB experience at state level. A second possibility is that over time this contradiction could lead to bureaucratisation, the emergence of a semiprofessional layer of PB experts in the communities, a decline in active participation, and disenchantment. Elements of this danger have already been felt.

But there is a third possibility – and this is the point of the radical conception of the PB. The PB has a dynamic that points towards a break with the existing framework. At the same time it can create the awareness and the social force needed for just such a rupture.

Obviously this could never happen in a single city or state. But some in the PT believed that much the same contradiction at national level, like that which faced the Lula government when it took office at the beginning of 2003 (symbolised by its twin commitments to honouring IMF targets and eradicating hunger), could begin to set the scene for such a break. They recognised that this could only happen if there were a big rise in social mobilisation and the development of a really credible alternative project. They suggested that the existing instruments of the PB and the demand for their extension across the board – alongside land occupations by the Landless Workers' Movement (MST) and the reactivation of radical trade unionism through the PT-linked trade union federation Single Workers' Centre (CUT) – could be the key strategic instruments the left in the PT would need to deploy.

But the signs so far are that the Lula government has abandoned that contradiction and reduced its twin commitments to one, namely the commitment to honour IMF targets. This has made the situation more complicated for the left. It looks increasingly unlikely that there will be any attempt to extend the PB across Brazil. An alternative might have to be built out of a combination of social mobilisations with merely local expressions of participatory democracy. The central contradiction, however, has not gone away. In the long run, the PB can still achieve its radical promise only if it moves forward, expands onto a higher level, and breaks through the constraints imposed on local government.

PT, participatory budget and transition to socialism

Here in the South we have shown it is possible to break the mould of the 'only possible way of thinking' and govern our city with participatory democracy and a capacity to invest.

We know the population wants more services and better services and that means taking on more staff, not the layoffs of the neoliberals' minimum state.

We have proved that public services and state enterprises can run a surplus when they are administered without corruption, with transparency and with democratic control by the population. To the erosion imposed by central government on the real wages of public sector workers, on pensions and on the minimum wage, we have responded with bimonthly adjustments to keep wages in line with inflation.

More fundamentally we have built a new relationship between state and society, which goes beyond representative democracy. The international recognition given the participatory budget is no accident. It has huge potential for a new understanding of democracy. Deepening it in practice, elaborating a fuller theoretical understanding, and making all this the shared property of the party as a whole are challenges still to be taken up in full.

The same audacity that allowed us to change, that built this participatory democracy, pushes us towards new confrontations. A programme of transition to socialism requires us to put forward at every moment proposals that can result in a qualitative leap in the activity and awareness of those involved.

Our utopia, the achievement of a socialist society, the thing that inspires us to keep going, cannot be the result of any decree or any belief in some magical moment in the future.

There are no 'maximum' and 'minimum' programmes. Our strategy is built out of conquests and achievements at the level of people's own awareness, which encourage them to struggle more and prepare them for future confrontations. Our strategy also grows out of a clear definition of which social classes we represent and what kind of alliances support that.

Our achievements in local government should not obscure the fundamental fact: achieving a socialist society is impossible without building another kind of state and another concept of property.

From '20 Years of the PT', a speech by Raul Pont on the occasion of the 20th anniversary of the founding of the Brazilian Workers' Party, March 2000.

PART II

How it Works

3
Basic Principles

Ubiratan de Souza[1]

Few people have been more closely involved in the PB at both municipal and state level than Ubiratan de Souza. In this chapter he looks at the universal characteristics of the Porto Alegre experience that made possible its extension to state level, and which in his view should also make possible its extension to national level.

For a decade and a half the participatory budget, or PB, has drawn the attention of civil society, local government leaders and academics. The process of participatory control developed around the PB is a revolutionary experiment. For that reason, all those who want to democratise power have followed it closely. For the same reason, it has spurred the resistance of those who prefer to see power concentrated.

The experience of participatory budgets over the last 15 years in Porto Alegre and various municipalities around Brazil and abroad, from Belo Horizonte, São Paulo and Recife to Cordoba in Spain and, between 1999 and 2002, the state government of Rio Grande do Sul have shown that this is a powerful instrument for distributing public money, democratising control of the local state and fostering active citizenship.

Clearly therefore there are some universal principles and lessons to be drawn from the PB, which are valid for this form of participatory democracy wherever it is applied and on whatever scale.

DIRECT DEMOCRACY

The PB is a process of direct, voluntary and universal democracy, where the population can discuss and decide on public policies and the public budget. The citizen's participation is not limited to the act of voting every four years; it goes much further, towards deciding on and controlling key aspects of public administration. The citizen ceases to be a simple adjunct of traditional politics, an occasional participant in occasional elections, and becomes a permanent protagonist of the public sphere.

The PB combines direct democracy with representative democracy, which is one of the great achievements of humanity and needs to be preserved and improved. Representative democracy is essential but insufficient in the process of deepening democracy in human society. More than ever we need to combine it with a whole variety of forms of direct democracy, where the citizen can not only participate actively in public administration but also control the state. The PB in the city of Porto Alegre and its extension to the state of Rio Grande do Sul are concrete examples of direct democracy.

BEYOND ACTUALLY EXISTING DEMOCRACY

Since the fall of the Berlin Wall, it has become clear that the Wall fell on both sides, to the East and to the West. The contemporary state faces a crisis of legitimacy, both political and fiscal. The liberal bourgeois state, in its current neoliberal phase, has sharpened the process of social exclusion. More and more human beings are concentrated in the most precarious living conditions in big urban centres. The total inadequacy of so-called 'compensatory' policies to deal with the problems of capitalist society has become obvious to everyone. The struggle against social exclusion demands public policies that change the distribution of income and power in our cities and across our countries, introducing forms of direct participation by the population in the administration of public affairs. That is why the PB is so widely recognised at home and abroad: because it responds to the challenges of modern times and, above all, to the contemporary state's crisis of legitimacy.

Our experience of the PB also points the way towards overcoming, in today's circumstances, the crisis of bureaucratic socialism. It provides a creative and original response to the main political aspect of the decay and failure in Eastern Europe, namely the autocratic relationship between the state and society.

UNIVERSAL PARTICIPATION

In the PB, citizens participate directly in decisionmaking and control of the public budget; they are not represented indirectly by other bodies. This direct participation of the population is free and universal, through public budget assemblies. It is this principle that makes the PB, with its decisionmaking powers, different from other traditional forms of popular consultation.

Every citizen, regardless of party, organisational or religious affiliation, is guaranteed the right to participate. Nobody enjoys privileges in the process of direct democracy and nobody is assured an elected place as PB delegate or councillor. This universal principle has ensured, during the 15 years of PB in Porto Alegre and its four years in Rio Grande do Sul state, that the process has never been taken over by any party or dominated by any corporation. It has ensured that the will of society can express itself in a plural and universal fashion.

This form of universal participation has encouraged citizens with no organisational links of any kind to go to the assemblies with their particular demands. The shared experience in the PB has often led these citizens to look for other ways of organising in their own communities, thereby strengthening the process of popular organisation. At the same time, those already organised in neighbourhood associations or other popular movements can mobilise their members to take part in the PB on an individual basis, to try to win support for their priorities and thus strengthen their own organisations. In fact the only ones who lose out with this kind of participation are the pseudo-leaders of phantom organisations, who claim to represent thousands of people but are unable to bring out even their own leaderships to argue for priorities and elect delegates.

THE WHOLE BUDGET

Another fundamental aspect of the PB process is that it discusses the whole budget and all public policies. The population's capacity to manage must not be underestimated. It must not be just a part of the budget that is singled out for discussion and deliberation. It is necessary to open up the budget in its entirety, including personnel costs, public debt, basic services, investments and related activities, development projects, as well as the extra-budgetary financial resources available through (for example) a state bank. In this way the population gradually takes charge of public spending and policies, creating the conditions for their effective participation in the public administration as a whole.

In this sense the local or state government should make all the facts relating to income and spending available to the population, and explain the technical aspects so that the population can really be in a position to analyse, decide and control the public budget. For example, in the Porto Alegre experience, the PB process created concrete mechanisms of control over the payroll, by setting up a tripartite commission (government, PB council and public employees' union) that discussed and decided on the creation of new council posts, exercising internal and external control over any increase in the workforce. There was also a growing awareness that investments in social areas like education and healthcare entail new costs (in wages and services), which need to be accompanied by an increase in public revenue through fair taxation.

BUILDING ON EXISTING POLITICAL RIGHTS

The Brazilian constitution says the public budget is the prerogative of the executive arm. This principle is repeated in the Rio Grande do Sul state constitution and in the municipal by-laws. However, the Brazilian Constitution also says, 'All power emanates from the people, who exercise it either through representatives or directly, in accordance with this constitution.' Elsewhere the Constitution affirms the 'right of assembly' and the 'right to petition public authorities', and a more recent Law on Fiscal Responsibility says that 'transparency will be ensured by promoting people's involvement in public meetings during the drawing up and discussion of budget plans and guidelines'.

Thus the elected government has the right to propose a budget and then send it to the elected local assembly, which turns it into law.

One of the merits of the process of direct democracy around the participatory budget is that it does not exclude these principles of representative democracy, but improves upon them. The elected assembly retains all its constitutional rights. It continues to analyse and vote on the proposed budget. For this reason, no new legislation is required to implement the PB. It requires only the political will of those elected via the mechanisms of representative democracy.

SELF-MANAGING, AUTONOMOUS AND OPEN

The PB process needs its own rules. These include criteria for the allocation of resources, and methods of planning. But these rules must be drawn up in complete autonomy by the community, which then makes a social contract with the local government. The PB is not a finished or perfect construct. It is, and must remain, open to discussion. Any claim to perfection would be an expression of authoritarianism. It would negate the dialectical process of constant mutation, of the new replacing the old, that characterises all social processes.

In this spirit, the government and the community should make a critical evaluation of the PB's rules and procedures every year. It should then be up to the PB council, operating in a self-governing, autonomous fashion with no interference from the executive or legislative branches of government, to discuss and decide any changes needed to bring these procedures up to date. This principle of self-regulation applied to the PB in Porto Alegre and Rio Grande do Sul state has resulted in constant modernisation of the democratic mechanisms of participatory planning.

For the PB to be a genuine and effective process of popular participation, not just a process of consultation, the decisions taken by the population and the government need to be documented and published so that they are available to everyone. In the case of Rio Grande do Sul, this record has taken the form of the 'Investment and Services Plan'. This gives the population the means to follow up and oversee the implementation of the works and services decided on. In addition, the government must provide a yearly account of its actions, in order to allow effective social control over the operations of the state.

SOLIDARITY, SELF-ESTEEM AND CONSCIOUS CITIZENSHIP

Direct participation by citizens in deciding priorities, drawing up the budget and the Investment and Services Plan, and controlling public affairs has made it possible to build a genuinely participatory form of planning, held together by a sense of solidarity. As a result, the PB has given birth to an awareness amongst citizens of their own capacity for freedom. This awareness is very different from anything promoted directly or indirectly through the media by some elite group. It is a result of ordinary citizens discovering the power of collective action. The shared experience of solidarity allows all citizens, at their own pace, to develop a critical awareness of society.

Once awakened, this awareness gives people a sense of their rights as citizens: rights to education, healthcare, a better quality of life, and other rights that go well beyond the reach of the local budget, which depend on broader struggles for structural changes in society and the economy. This awareness and widespread sense of solidarity have also led to the recognition within the PB of the rights and needs of minority groups. These processes go together to produce a new relationship between individual citizens and their communities within the PB, a new relationship of respect and public recognition. This in turn leads to greater self-esteem and self-confidence, often amongst people from the most marginalised and oppressed sections of society.

Throughout history we have seen how bureaucracy develops not only within the state, but also within social movements and organisations. Relations between leaders and their grassroots also require participatory mechanisms of accountability and control.

The experience of the PB has played a strategic role in democratising social relations, both within the state and outside it. The PB is a permanent effort to promote democratic participation and control in trade unions, social movements and other grassroots organisations as well as in political parties.

4
Porto Alegre: The City Budget

André Passos Cordeiro[1]

The people of Thebes! Since when do I take my orders from the
people of Thebes?

Creon, king of Thebes, in Sophocles' *Antigone*[2]

Our era has been marked by an increasing disbelief in politics. There
is a widespread view that formal political institutions are impotent
or distant from social reality, or act as bulwarks against social and
economic change of any kind. This is expressed in electoral abstention
in those countries where voting is voluntary, and even in some where
it is not (as in the huge number of abstentions, blank and spoiled
votes in Argentina that preceded the fall of the de la Rua government
at the end of 2001). Participation is seen as incapable of generating
major changes.

Thus, paradoxically, while the idea of 'democracy' is promoted
worldwide as the best form of government, in practice the classic
political system of representative democracy shows signs of
exhaustion. In a market society, without any sort of direct social
control over elected representatives, the state becomes an easy prey
to private interests.

Two central tasks have to be undertaken, therefore. Firstly, society's
confidence in the state's ability to act as a tool of social change needs
to be restored. Secondly, there is a need to develop autonomous
processes in society itself that permanently produce such change.
Confidence may be restored with or without a recovery of citizens'
political participation, but permanent social mechanisms of change
require real participation. Throughout history there are examples of
the state acting as an agent of significant material change – reducing
poverty levels for example – but at the same time aggravating even
more the phenomenon of depoliticisation and alienation. This kind
of political practice reduces state action to a set of compensatory
policies counteracting the damage done by the economic system.
Politics remains subordinated to economics. Not a scratch is made
on the predominant tendency to apathy and selfishness.

To reverse this logic, it is necessary to stimulate the initiative and self-organisation of the majority of the population. Direct citizen participation through the participatory budget (PB) in managing public resources and deciding the direction of state actions paves the way for building a new kind of political system. By combining direct decisionmaking by the people about general priorities with a system of delegates with revocable mandates overseeing the details, the PB establishes a new plateau for democratic practice. Any citizen who wants to can take part, from shaping the rules to deciding local government's priorities. The people can be sure that their decisions will be respected, and that otherwise both city hall and their own representatives in the PB can be held to account.

The result is that the traditional logic for distributing public resources – based on vested economic interests and electoral advantage – is turned on its head. In its place a planning method emerges that makes it possible to reduce social deprivation by providing infrastructure and services to areas of the city formerly cut off from them, while at the same time establishing priorities for major public works that benefit the whole city.

Finally, the participatory budget has proved that it is possible to rescue the true role of representation. This means representatives working to ensure implementation of the priorities directly decided by those they represent. Both direct democracy and representative democracy have their place. The people of Thebes should indeed be giving Creon his orders.

A BRIEF HISTORY

Porto Alegre, the capital of Rio Grande do Sul State, is a city of 1,360,590 inhabitants. It is at the centre of a metropolitan region with a population of about 3 million. Porto Alegre grew rapidly in the 1980s and experienced a sharp concentration of income. As a result nearly a third of the population moved to areas with little or no infrastructure.

The popular administration came to office in 1989 with Olívio Dutra's election as mayor. Up until then, city hall had suffered from a series of administrations that had built relationships with the population based on corruption and patronage, without any kind of transparency. Decisions on investments did not take account of the real needs of the majority, who were excluded from much of the city's life. Some 98 per cent of the city's revenue went to pay employees' wages. There was an immense social debt and few resources to address the community's problems and needs.

A sweeping tax reform was necessary to increase the amount of resources available for investment and begin to tackle the social debt to those suffering extreme deprivation. Tax reform, together with the beginnings of the participatory budget (PB), led to continuous improvement in the quality of life in Porto Alegre, shaped by the decisions of the population as a whole.

Participation was initially low, until the tax reform began to produce results and make it possible really to implement the decisions taken by the population. As capacity to invest was restored, participation began to grow.

The number of people taking part in the participatory budget has been growing, year after year, as Table 4.1 shows.

Table 4.1 Participation in Porto Alegre participatory budget, 1990–2001

Year	Total attendance at Regional meetings*	Total attendance at Thematic meetings**
1990	976	
1991	3694	
1992	7610	
1993	10735	
1994	9638	1609
1995	11821	2446
1996	10148	1793
1997	11908	4105
1998	13688	2769
1999	16813	3911
2000	15331	3694
2001	18583	3222

Note: These figures do not include those taking part in the smaller, less formal, neighbourhood meetings, for which no attendance details are registered. The total number of people taking part in the participatory budget each year may therefore be as much as twice the numbers recorded above.

* The regional meetings take place in Porto Alegre's 16 regions: Ilhas, Humaitá, East, Lomba, North, Northeast, Partenon, Restinga, Glória, Cruzeiro, Cristal, South Centre, Far South, Eixo Baltazar, South and Centre.

** The thematic meetings, first held in 1994, cover the six fields: transport and traffic; health and social services; education, sports and leisure; culture (since 2000); economic development and taxation; and city organisation and urban development.

The number of neighbourhood associations and similar bodies registered with the PB has grown in the same way, to about 1,000 today.

Widespread respect for PB decisions has had a significant impact on municipal revenues. It has for example made it easier to overcome the tax evasion that has often been endemic in Brazil. Today in Porto Alegre, unlike many other municipalities, the revenue from locally raised taxes accounts for more than 50 per cent of the total. This is largely because it is easy to see where and how the money is being spent and, most importantly, because decisions are being taken by the population.

The participatory budget has allowed the population to identify which demands should be dealt with first. It has produced an inversion of priorities compared with those of previous administrations, and has helped to redress a significant part of the social debt.

Porto Alegre now has 99 per cent of its population supplied with treated water and 83 per cent connected to the sewage system. In 1988, when the PT was first elected, barely 50 per cent were connected to the sewage system. Since then, more than 250 kilometres of the city's roads and streets have been made up, including asphalt and drains, mainly in the poorest neighbourhoods. Public spending on housing rose more than fourfold between 1989 and 2000. In the same period the number of municipal-run schools increased in about the same proportion, from 22 to 90, while the failure rate among school students fell from 30 per cent to 10 per cent. Some 114 new community-run creches began receiving local government funding, where before there had been none. Porto Alegre's municipal bus company was the first in Brazil to operate vehicles with full wheelchair access.

The PB has been adopted in a number of cities across Brazil and been globally recognised by the United Nations[3] as an exemplary method of public administration.

SPACES FOR PARTICIPATION

The fundamental point about the participatory budget in Porto Alegre is that it is not the local government and its experts who draw up the municipal budget and investment plan, but the population, in consultation with officials and experts. We can therefore identify three different kinds of space in which the PB operates.

First and most important, there are two ways in which the population as a whole can participate directly in discussing and shaping the Porto Alegre public budget: either territorially, in the regions where they live; or thematically, within particular subject areas.

Territorially, the city is divided into 16 regions, with the boundaries drawn up – through an agreement between local government and the community movement – to take account of political and cultural affinities between different sectors. In the main regional meetings, the people select their top four priorities for spending out of a list of 14 budget headings. At present this list comprises: sewers and drains, housing, social services, paving, water supply, education, street lighting, health, transport, leisure areas, sports and leisure, economic development, culture, and environmental improvement. However, the list may be changed from one year to the next by decision of the PB process itself. In smaller local meetings, the population draws up an order of priority, or hierarchy, for the specific works and services they are demanding in their area, in line with the four prioritised budget headings. In other words, the various regional meetings of the PB tend to focus on the local needs of different neighbourhoods.

In the thematic meetings, priorities of a more global character are selected. There is a broader discussion of the needs of the city as a whole. These thematic meetings were introduced into the PB in Porto Alegre in the mid 1990s, partly in an effort to address these more general issues and partly in an effort to involve sections of the population that had not played a very active part in the PB up until then – including trade unionists, trades people and small businesses, students, cultural movements and environmentalists.

In both regional and thematic meetings, delegates are elected to the delegate forum – there is one forum for each region and each thematic area – and councillors are elected to the citywide participatory budget council.

Thus, in addition to the open public assemblies where everyone can participate, the PB has created several permanent, representative structures. Here the elected PB delegates and councillors discuss and decide on different aspects of how to implement the general decisions taken through the direct participation of the population. The most important permanent structure is the PB council, which has overall responsibility for running the PB process. It meets twice a week throughout the year and has the job of combining and reconciling the priorities and demands put forward by the different regions and thematic areas into a coherent whole, and ensuring that the decisions of the population are carried out. The various delegate forums meet at least once a month and have the principal task, within each geographical or thematic area, of turning the generic list of priorities voted by the open assemblies into concrete demands for specific works and services in specific streets or neighbourhoods. There are also more ad hoc bodies set up, such as service forums and works commissions, to oversee and support different aspects of the PB's implementation.

Finally, local government also participates in this discussion process, but it does not have a vote. In the various meetings of the regions and thematic areas, different local government departments present proposals and provide basic and vital information to improve the quality of the discussion. The city hall planning cabinet and finance department present the estimated headline figures for income and spending in the year to come.

FIVE STAGES

The annual cycle of the participatory budget can be divided into five main stages: the preparatory meetings; the single round of regional and thematic assemblies; the municipal assembly; presentation of the investment plan to the delegate forums; discussion and voting on the PB rules and technical criteria (for the following year).

(1) Preparatory meetings

The first phase of the cycle, the preparatory meetings, happens within each region and thematic area in the months of March and April. The exact number and form of these 'micro-regional' meetings can vary and are decided locally – they may correspond to a particular neighbourhood, street or group of streets. Anyone living in that area can attend. These meetings are a first chance for the population to hold the local government to account for its performance in the previous year, to review what has been agreed for the current year, and to begin the process of discussing what should be done next year.

At these relatively informal meetings, representatives of city hall first report on the extent to which the previous year's activities succeeded in fulfilling the investment plan agreed by the PB the year before last. There is a critical discussion of this. There is also a presentation of the investment plan already agreed for this year, and of any changes agreed to the PB's internal rules and procedures which may affect the way the discussion of the coming year's budget will be conducted.

The meetings then begin the discussion of priorities for this coming budget. They also discuss how they want to draw up slates for the election of the councillors who will sit on this year's participatory budget council.

There is a coordinating committee that helps to organise these micro-regional meetings. It is made up of one representative from the city hall's planning cabinet, the head of the community relations co-ordinating group, the PB coordinator for that region and the PB councillors elected to the previous year's PB council from that region or thematic area.

This initial phase of the cycle also begins to register the suggestions for priorities and specific investments sent in by the Internet.

(2a) Regional and thematic assemblies

These open, public assemblies are the heart of the PB process. It is here, at the beginning of the second phase of the cycle, that the population discusses and decides its priorities for how city hall's money should be spent, and elects the PB councillors who will turn these priorities into detailed spending plans.

Up until the year 2001, this part of the PB was spread across two rounds of meetings. Starting in 2002, the PB council decided to make the process simpler and more accessible. It combined the functions into a single round of regional and thematic assemblies, held from April to May, at the end of the preparatory meetings. This change was a lesson learnt directly from the experience of how the participatory budget had begun to be applied at state level in Rio Grande do Sul.[4]

These assemblies – 16 regional ones and six thematic ones – are open to the public. All citizens can take part, either in the regions where they live or in the thematic areas of their choice. The meetings are publicised well in advance on TV and radio, with posters, leaflets and loudspeaker cars driving round the neighbourhoods. The numbers attending each assembly can vary from 400 or 500 to over 1,500.

A team of staff laid on by city hall carefully registers everyone attending, taking down details of name, address and the particular neighbourhood, zone or residents' association the address relates to, before handing over voting credentials and ballot forms. This is important, both to prevent any abuse of the system and because it will later provide the basis for calculating the numbers of delegates to be elected to the regional delegate forums from each neighbourhood – one delegate for every ten citizens from that neighbourhood attending this main regional assembly.

While registration is underway, a brief cultural activity – some music or a clown show put on by a local group – helps warm up the atmosphere. Each assembly then begins with a representative of local government explaining the procedures, including any changes agreed since the previous year. Then a representative of the finance department gives an outline, on the overhead projector, of how much money is available for the budget about to be discussed, based on projected local tax revenues, central government transfers and so forth. There is then time for 15 speakers from the floor, taken on a first-come first-served basis, each with three minutes to argue in favour of a particular set of priorities. To make it easier for everyone to follow, all the speakers are filmed and projected live onto one or two giant screens.

The assembly then votes on its priorities for next year's budget. Each citizen present lists in order of his or her first four choices from the list of 14 budget headings.

As the process of filling in the ballot forms gets underway, the mayor of Porto Alegre, who attends all these regional and thematic assemblies and has been listening to the proceedings so far, delivers his account of the way the local administration has been faring and the challenges ahead. He will generally try to take up the main points made from the floor, but he plays no part in the voting process and his speech is not intended to suggest how people should or should not vote. Rather it is meant to ensure that the mayor keeps in touch with the participatory process and is seen to be taking account of the criticisms and suggestions coming from the communities.

In this latter part of the assembly, the communities also elect their councillors to the PB council. There are two councillors and two substitutes for each of the 16 regions and six thematic areas. In line with the PB's own internal rules, their mandate is for one year, with only one re-election allowed. If the community is dissatisfied with any councillor's performance, the forum of delegates for that region or thematic area can revoke the mandate at any time.

The election of the councillors is organised by slates. When there is more than one slate, the one with the largest vote will get one councillor for each 25 per cent of the vote, beginning with the full councillors and continuing with the substitutes. The other councillors will then be allocated according to the percentages won by each of the other slates.

In addition to the 32 councillors elected from the regional assemblies and the 12 from the thematic assemblies (plus their substitutes), there is one councillor and a substitute nominated by the Municipal Workers' Trade Union and another by the Union of Neighbourhood Associations (UAMPA). All these councillors have the right both to speak and vote on the PB council.

The coordinator of the city hall planning cabinet and the head of the community relations coordinating group – nominated by the mayor – are also members of the PB council, with the right to speak but with no right to vote.

The PB council has the main responsibility for discussing and deciding all aspects of the city's spending plans, always respecting the general priorities and specific demands expressed by the population. This means that, in the words of the PB's own statutes, the PB council has the power to 'consider, evaluate, approve, disapprove and alter, in part or in its entirety', every element of the city budget, including the multi-year plan, the budget guidelines law, the budget proposal, the investment plan and the taxation policy. However, in line with the Brazilian Constitution, most of these statutory instruments, and especially the annual public budget proposal itself, have to be submitted to the city council[5] for final approval.

(2b) Regional and thematic forums

After the single round of regional and thematic assemblies, this second phase of the PB cycle continues from May through June and July, with another series of smaller, local meetings, self-organised by neighbourhood, street, or thematic area. Again each community decides the number and the form of the meetings according to its political, geographical and cultural characteristics.

These meetings elect each neighbourhood or area's delegates to the various regional and thematic delegate forums, according to the proportions explained above – one delegate for every ten people from that neighbourhood or area who attended the main assembly. They also begin to prepare a list of specific works and services demanded by that neighbourhood or area.

The delegates then visit the locations of these different demands – the particular street that needs paving, or group of houses that needs improved drains – before returning to work with the community in drawing up an order of priority, or 'hierarchy of demands', for the specific works and services that neighbourhood or area wants included in next year's investment plan.

Representatives of the different municipal departments feed technical information about the feasibility and implications of different proposals into these discussions. They may also themselves put forward proposals for discussion.

The delegates therefore have the job of elaborating and coordinating the investment and service plans together with local government, in accordance with the overall priorities decided directly by the population at the main assemblies. In order to carry out these responsibilities, they form in each region and thematic area a delegate forum, in which the relevant PB councillors also take part.

(3) Municipal assembly

The third phase is marked by the next big meeting in the cycle, the municipal assembly, held in July, usually in one of the city's main amphitheatres or sports arenas. This is where the PB councillors elected in the regional and thematic assemblies are sworn in, and where the detailed lists of priorities for works and services drawn up in the different regional and thematic forums are presented to the local government. It is also where the planning cabinet and the finance department present the main budget headings for next year's spending (wages, overheads, contracted services, investment, and so on) on behalf of the mayor's office, as well as an estimate of next year's revenue.

This whole discussion is carefully minuted and the demands coming from the regional and thematic forums are recorded on special forms. One set of forms gives the details of each particular work or service proposed by each of the regions, as shown in Figure 4.1 (see pages 74–5).

This starts by identifying the region concerned, which of the four budget priorities voted on by the regional assembly the particular demand corresponds to, and the position of this demand in that region's overall order of preferences. The form then goes on to give a detailed description of the particular work or service demanded, its location and extent. In the case of infrastructure projects like sanitation and paving a grid map is included to show the exact streets or blocks that will be covered.

Another set of forms gives details of the sectoral priorities coming from each of the thematic forums and their order of preference.

(4) Final budget and investment plan

In the fourth phase of the cycle, from July to December, all these lists of priorities and demands are used to draw up the two main instruments coming out of the PB: first the budget framework and then the investment plan. To begin with, city hall makes a technical and financial analysis of the demands it has received and develops a framework for the budget and the distribution of resources among the different regions and thematic areas. This budget framework is discussed and voted on at the PB council in August and September. The end result is then written up as the annual public budget proposal and submitted to the city council for ratification.

After this a similar procedure is followed to draw up the investment and services plan. City hall develops a proposal on the basis of its technical and financial analysis of the demands presented. This then goes back to the regions and thematic areas for discussion, giving the population as much chance as possible to make alterations and propose alternatives, while the experts can try to explain why they think certain demands may not be feasible either technically or financially. Finally, the regional and thematic delegate forums vote on the plan.

(5) Changing the rules

In the fifth and last phase, from November to January, first the delegate forums and then the PB council discuss any suggested changes to the participatory budget rules and technical criteria. The PB council then votes on whether to adopt any of these changes for the next PB cycle, which is about to begin. In February – a month of holidays and carnival in Brazil – the PB council goes into recess.

Let us now look in more detail at how these two central pillars of the local government's spending plans – the annual public budget proposal and the investment and services plan – are prepared and decided.

PLANNING INDICATORS

The municipal planning cabinet drafts the two documents referred to above on the basis of three basic planning indicators:

(1) the priorities chosen by the population in the regions;
(2) the guidelines for works and services selected by the population in the thematic areas, along with the long-term projects and structural works already in process;
(3) the local government's obligation to maintain certain levels of core services for the population as well as emergency provisions.

DEMAND FORM

PARTICIPATORY BUDGET 2003
GAPLAN - Planning Cabinet

Prefeitura de Porto Alegre
ADMINISTRAÇÃO POPULAR

ORCAMENTO
PARTICIPATIVO

REGION:

Region's Code

Region's Name

BUDGET PRIORITY:

Which of the Region's 4 Budget Priorities this Demand Falls Within

HIERARCHY:

Where this Demand Falls in Region's Order of Preferences

DEMAND DESCRIPTION

(**Complete with the kind of service needed, its location, extension and a reference point)**

SUB-THEME:

Thematic Priority Sub-Theme's Name

DESCRIPTION:

START POINT

(Complete only for Paving, Drainage, Sewers and Water)

END POINT

(Complete only for Paving, Drainage, Sewers and wate Water)

EXTENSION NEEDED:

Extension i in metres - Paving, Drains, Sewers and Water

NEIGHBOURHOOD

Neighborhood's name

BLOCK/STREETS

Name of Block or Street

DEMANDED BY WHO:

TO BE USED BY GAPLAN

DEMAND CODE: 2 0 0 3

PRIORITY	PROGRAMME	HIERARCHY
DATE	NEIGHBORHOOD	BLOCK
DEPARTMENT	REGION	
ZIP CODE		

Porto Alegre City Hall - R Record of Receipt

| Councillor - 2002 | Councillor - 2002 | GAPLAN | / / DATE |

NOTES:
1. Demands must be delivered by the Municipal Assembly
2. Last chance to change/correct demands: 02/08/2002
3. Councillors must sign the Demand Forms
4. Demand Forms without the Councillors' signatures will not be accepted
5. Demands for paving, sewers, water and drains need the location map

LOCATION MAP

COMPLETE THE FORM WITH THE NAMES OF THE NEAREST STREETS, IN ORDER TO GIVE A REFERENCE POINT

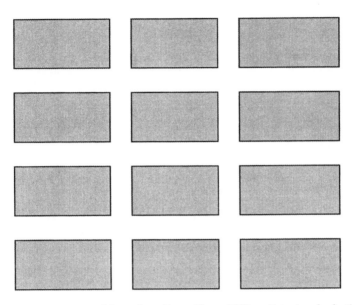

Figure 4.1   Demand form (from Porto Alegre 2003 participatory budget)

The priorities of the regions are chosen from 14 different budget headings. As we have already seen, the community in each of the regional assemblies chooses four of them and delivers them to the planning cabinet in the municipal assembly. A points system is used to calculate an overall order of priorities, as shown in Table 4.2.

First priority	4 points
Second priority	3 points
Third priority	2 points
Fourth priority	1 point

By adding the points from each region, the priorities are established for the city as a whole. The three budget categories with the highest total number of points become the three top priorities for all 16 regions of the city. The distribution of resources for works and services in all the regions is decided accordingly.

The thematic guidelines (or sectoral policy priorities) are identified from the priority forms delivered by the six thematic plenaries and

Table 4.2 Regional priorities (from Porto Alegre 2003 participatory budget)

Region	Sewers and Drains	Water Supply	Housing	Paving	Education	Social Services	Health	Transport	Leisure Areas	Sports and Leisure	Street Lighting	Economic Development	Culture	Environmental Improvement
Humaitá/ Navegantes/Ilhas			4		1	3						2		
Northwest	1		4		3	2								
East			2	1	3	2	2							
Lomba Do Pinheiro			3	4	3									
North	2	1	4	2	1									
Northeast			3	4	2							1		
Partenon		2	4		1	1	2							
Restinga			4		4	1						1		
Glória			4	2	3		1							
Cruzeiro			4		3	2	1							
Cristal			4		2	3						1		
Central-South	1		4	3			2							
Far-South	3	3		4										
Eixo Baltazar		2	4		2		2							
South	3		2	4		1								
Centre			4		2	3	1							
Total	10	8	54	24	30	18	11	0	0	0	0	5	0	0

Note: Points per category chosen by each region

Citywide total for each category

Housing	54 points	Economic development	5 points
Education	30 points	Leisure areas	0 points
Paving	24 points	Sports and leisure	0 points
Social services	18 points	Street lighting	0 points
Health	11 points	Transport	0 points
Sewers and drains	10 points	Culture	0 points
Water supply	8 points	Environmental improvement	0 points

forums, as already mentioned. The longer-term, structural works and services already underway – projects that were part of some previous investment plan and require continuing finance in order to keep going – are identified from the planning cabinet's own project management system.

The third indicator, the government's need to maintain a certain level of basic services, refers to that part of local government resources already committed to spending on education, health, clean water, refuse collection and the like. These expenses account for a significant part of the city's revenue and are comparatively rigid. They could only be altered over the medium or long term. This third indicator also includes the need to direct a portion of resources to emergency expenditures of one sort or another.

Working with these three indicators, and an estimate of income provided by the municipal finance department, the planning cabinet draws up a first budget framework. After discussion and elaboration in the city finance committee, the mayor's coordinating team and each city hall department, this framework is sent for discussion at the PB council during September. Here the full details of the proposed services and investments in each area are spelt out. The PB council has the power to change the allocation of resources (in theory it could change the entire budget) if it thinks that would better meet the priorities decided by the population.

Once the PB council has approved the budget, the planning cabinet writes it up as the final, official annual public budget proposal, which in line with the Brazilian constitution has to be presented to the city council for its approval.

After the budget proposal goes to the city council, the PB council begins the process of deciding on the plan for investments and services.

This investment plan is based on:

(1) the budget proposal given to the City Council;
(2) the technical, legal and financial analysis of the demands listed in order of preference by the communities in the different regions;
(3) the 'general criteria' for the allocation of resources between the regions.

These general criteria for the allocation of resources set the quantity of resources that goes to each region for investments and services *in the first three global priority categories* (that is the categories that come out in first, second and third place when the points from all 16 regions are added together – see Table 4.2). For the 2003 budget, that meant housing, education and paving, in that order. The 'general criteria' are of three kinds, each with a different value, as shown in Table 4.3.

Table 4.4 below shows how this system works, using the specific example of resources for paving in the 2003 participatory budget. For each region the points are multiplied by the value, and the resulting numbers are added together to reach a final score for each region in that particular budget category (in this case paving). The PB council decided the total quantity of resources available across the city for paving when it voted on the budget framework, as described above. That total quantity is now divided amongst the regions in the proportions indicated by their final score according to these three general criteria.

Table 4.3   General criteria for Porto Alegre participatory budget

Total population of region	
Value 2	
Up to 25,000 inhabitants	1 point
25,001 to 45,000 inhabitants	2 points
45,001 to 90,000 inhabitants	3 points
More than 90,001 inhabitants	4 points
Lack of service or infrastructure	
Value 4	
0.01 per cent to 14.99 per cent	1 point
15 per cent to 50.99 per cent	2 points
51 per cent to 75.99 per cent	3 points
More than 76 per cent	4 points
Priority voted by region	
Value 5	
Fourth priority	1 points
Third priority	2 points
Second priority	3 points
First priority	4 points

As a result the regions that have the greatest shortage of paving, the largest populations and have voted the greatest priority to paving in their assemblies will get the largest share of the resources available

Table 4.4 Distribution of resources: paving (from Porto Alegre 2003 investment plan)

Region	Regional Priority			Infrastructure Needs			Population			Total	Resources	
	Points	Value	Total 1	Points	Value	Total 2	Points	Value	Total 3	(1 + 2 + 3)	%	(M)
Humaitá/Navegantes/Ilhas	0	5	0	1	4	4	3	2	6	10	3.16	269
Northwest	0	5	0	1	4	4	4	2	8	12	3.80	323
East	1	5	5	1	4	4	4	2	8	17	5.38	457
Lomba Do Pinheiro	4	5	20	2	4	8	3	2	6	34	10.76	915
North	0	5	0	1	4	4	4	2	8	12	3.80	323
Northeast	2	5	10	2	4	8	2	2	4	22	6.96	592
Partenon	4	5	20	1	4	4	4	2	8	32	10.13	861
Restinga	0	5	0	1	4	4	3	2	6	10	3.16	269
Glória	2	5	10	2	4	8	3	2	6	24	7.59	646
Cruzeiro	0	5	0	1	4	4	3	2	6	10	3.16	269
Cristal	0	5	0	1	4	4	2	2	4	8	2.53	215
Central-South	3	5	15	2	4	8	4	2	8	31	9.81	834
Far-South	4	5	20	3	4	12	2	2	4	36	11.39	968
Eixo Baltazar	0	5	0	2	4	8	4	2	8	16	5.06	430
South	4	5	20	1	4	4	3	2	6	30	9.49	807
Centre	0	5	0	1	4	4	4	2	8	12	3.80	323
General Total										316	100.00	8501

for paving. The implementation of the priorities will first occur in regions that selected that particular priority among the first four.

These general criteria for the allocation of resources between the regions are only applied to the first three global priorities. For the remaining priorities the resources available will go in the first place to those regions that have made this one of their top four choices.

The investment plan therefore presents a detailed list of the works and services to be implemented by local government. The decision on exactly which works will be implemented is based on: (a) the availability of resources for each region; (b) where each project comes in the hierarchy of preferences decided by each community; (c) the project's cost; and (d) a technical analysis of the project's viability.

Once the PB council has approved the final investment plan, the process of drawing up the public budget through the PB has come to an end. The community's discussion and participation then turns towards monitoring local government's execution of the projects and priorities selected through the PB.

Table 4.5 presents a summary of how the participatory budget works in Porto Alegre.

And of course the cycle begins again.

Table 4.5 Summary of how the participatory budget works in Porto Alegre

March–April Phase 1	Preparatory meetings	In regions, micro-regions (neighbourhoods, streets, groups of streets, etc.) and thematic areas	Open to the public in general	Balance sheet of previous year; Presentation of this year's Investment Plan; Presentation of Rules and Criteria for deciding next year's budget; Initial discussion of priorities for next budget; Discussion of criteria for election of PB Councillors; Suggestion of priorities and demands via Internet	Regional assemblies select top four priorities from list of 14. Thematic assemblies have a more flexible scheme for choosing sectoral priorities
Mid April–May Phase 2a	Single round of regional and thematic assemblies	In 16 geographical regions and six thematic areas	Open to the public in general	Vote to choose priorities for next year's spending; Election of councillors to serve on incoming participatory budget council; Decide number of delegates to be elected to regional and thematic forums	Two full councillors and two substitutes elected for each region and thematic area by slate system. The number of delegates to be elected later to these forums is determined by the number of people from each neighbourhood or thematic sub-group attending this main assembly – one delegate for every ten of those present

Table 4.5 continued

May–July Phase 2b	Regional and thematic forums	Variety of meetings back in regions, micro-regions (neighbourhoods, streets, groups of streets, etc.) and thematic areas and sub-areas	Some open to public in general, others for delegates and councillors elected by public	Election of delegates from neighbourhoods etc. to regional and thematic delegate forums. Selection of works and services demanded in each region and thematic area and organisation of these in order of preference (hierarchy). Local government departments provide technical information needed by communities for their discussions. Demands submitted by the Internet are discussed by the delegates elected in each region and thematic area. Delegates visit site of demands	These delegates form the delegate forum for that region or thematic area. Each community organises its own meetings, as it sees fit, to discuss and decide the specific investments it wants in its area, in line with the four overall priorities decided at the main assembly. Before the 'hierarchy of demands' is finalised the delegates visit the location of each proposed project to get a better understanding of the need, feasibility, etc.
Mid July Phase 3	Municipal assembly	One large citywide meeting	Open to all members of public	Newly elected councillors take up positions on PB council	44 full councillors from the regions and thematic areas, one each from the Union of Neighbourhood Associations and the Municipal Workers' Trade Union, and two representatives of the mayor's office with voice but no vote.

July–September Phase 4a	Series of meetings between city hall departments and of PB council	Hierarchy of demands for works and services delivered to city hall	The regions deliver to the planning cabinet a form with the details of each work or service demanded. The thematic areas deliver a single form with their priority guidelines etc.
Preparing the budget framework	Involving first city hall staff, then elected PB councillors	General discussion of budget City hall prepares draft budget proposal	Planning cabinet analyses priorities and demands from regions and thematic areas and draws up first initial budget framework City hall departments draw up departmental spending plans on basis of initial budget framework Planning cabinet readjusts departmental plans to ensure they reflect priorities decided by population, then sends new budget proposal to PB council
		PB council discusses, alters and finalises budget proposal Final budget proposal sent to the elected city council for final approval	Elected councillors have the power to change part or all of the budget proposal if they believe that would better reflect the priorities decided directly by the population This is a requirement of the Brazilian Constitution. In practice the city council does not attempt to interfere with the budget finalised by the planning cabinet

Table 4.5 continued

October–December Phase 4b	Preparing the investment plan	Series of meetings in city hall, and in regions and thematic areas	Involving city hall staff, public in general and elected delegates	City hall prepares draft investment and services plan Regions and thematic areas discuss proposed investment plan Regional and thematic delegate forums discuss and decide final investment plan, which is then finally approved by the PB council	This is drawn up on the basis of the agreed budget proposal and the various criteria explained in this chapter Representatives of city hall – planning cabinet and community relations – also take part in these discussions
November–January Phase 5	Discussing and changing the rules	Series of meetings in regions and thematic areas then in PB council	Public in general then PB councillors	Decentralised meetings in neighbourhoods etc. to discuss and propose changes to the way the participatory budget operates PB council considers proposals and decides any rule changes for the next cycle of the participatory budget (PB)	

5
The Participatory Budget in Two Other Cities

Many other local administrations in Brazil and beyond have taken up the participatory budget, and applied it in many different ways. Some are far from radical; some claim to be revolutionary. One often cited as a successful example of applying the participatory budget in an innovative and radical way is Caxias do Sul, Rio Grande do Sul's third largest city. In the second part of this chapter, Caxias do Sul mayor Pepe Vargas explains how the PT there is trying to move beyond involving the population in merely deciding each year's budget, towards a form of popular participation in planning the city's longer-term future.

The city of Araraquara, in the north central part of São Paulo state, shares a number of characteristics with Caxias do Sul. A medium-sized provincial city of around 200,000 inhabitants in the middle of the country's most important orange-growing region, it too has a relatively high average income by Brazilian standards, with a significant industrial base and an extensive rural sector within its municipal boundaries. Also like Caxias do Sul, it has a mayor from the left of the PT. Edinho Silva[1] became mayor of Araraquara in January 2001. As he explains in this interview with Iain Bruce, the PT has borrowed much in Araraquara from the experience of the PB in Caxias do Sul, but has tried to innovate in other ways as well.

THE EXPERIENCE IN ARARAQUARA
Iain Bruce, interview with Edinho Silva

As soon as we won the elections in October 2000 we began a series of discussions to decide our priorities. We settled on three main areas – popular participation, policies to promote social inclusion, and a more efficient delivery of services to the population. In this latter area we wanted to wrest back the idea of modernity from the right, and show that it was possible to apply measures of efficiency and technology with a completely different logic – to promote popular interests. But of course the first two, popular participation and social inclusion, were to be our strategic priorities. Popular participation had two main aspects, the participatory budget and municipal councils.

Social inclusion was centred on the idea of workers' self-organisation – that is, that workers are capable of organising themselves to generate jobs and income without depending on the whims of capital. So, for example, we've encouraged the formation of cooperatives. One of them, a recycling cooperative formed by families who used to live on the council rubbish tip sorting through garbage, has now become the basis of the city hall's recycling programme and has won national recognition.

These two areas then – popular participation and social inclusion – were the strategic axes because they were the ones which, within a capitalist society, could show the city as a whole that it *is* possible to build relations of power based on very different ideas. We had a long debate on what kind of popular participation we wanted to promote.

How much power do these municipal councils have to make decisions, say about where a new bus route should go?

The city hall does what the people's municipal council says.

It's obliged to?

Yes, and we've already lost a number of arguments in the transport users' council – areas we really didn't think were priorities for new routes, but the council insisted ... and the town hall had to carry out their decision.

It's the same in health and education. We've set up users' councils for each hospital and health centre, and for each school. So we've adopted a model in which the city hall administration stimulates popular organisation, and popular organisations have decisionmaking powers and are autonomous.

The people's municipal councils are separate from the participatory budget process, because we realised that the PB cannot cope with all the population's demands. The participatory budget is not a panacea that can solve all problems. There are some services that need to be managed on a permanent, day-to-day basis, by the population.

Aren't there likely to be conflicts between these municipal councils and the participatory budget process?

Not really, because the municipal councils are management councils. The transport council can demand a new bus route for a neighbourhood that's not properly served. But it can't demand that the road to that neighbourhood be asphalted. That's a question of investment and has to go through the participatory budget. So the members of the transport council are likely to take that demand into their PB assembly, and the two things intersect. But in the meantime the buses on the new route will have to make do with the dirt track that exists at the moment. It's the same with a programme we have developed to bring local government closer to the people. We call it 'the town hall in the neighbourhoods'. Every week the local government departments – health, education, transport, environment and so on – move into a particular neighbourhood, and attend to the public there on the spot, so people don't feel they have to come into the city centre to be dealt with.

Obviously in the process people come up with many demands for particular investments – we need such and such built – and we have to explain, 'No! Budget matters have to be taken to your participatory budget assembly.' So it's an educational process. In the first year 5,000 people took part in the PB, out of a population of 200,000.

So with initiatives like this, as well as with the cooperatives I mentioned before, we were looking for ways of building a structure of alternative power within the existing society. We had big theoretical debates, among our PT members and supporters, about what would be the basic principles of a socialist society. We wanted to create the conditions for workers to be able to organise themselves, to break with the subordination of their labour, and show that it is possible for civil society to *control* the state. This alternative power structure is a way for us to begin to democratise the state.

So our approach to the participatory budget fitted into this. There's been a lot of debate within the PT, but we decided the PB should have decisionmaking powers over 100 per cent of the municipal investment budget.

So what's the debate?

In many PT municipalities the PB does not decide 100 per cent of the investments. In others it doesn't have decisionmaking powers at all. It's merely consultative. In other words it simply expresses an opinion about where the town hall should spend its money, but in the end local government decides. And there are other, mixed variants. But we went for 100 per cent of the budget from the very first year.

Our model was based on the one applied in Caxias do Sul in Rio Grande do Sul state, but we've changed some things. It's not that there are big differences with Porto Alegre – that's obviously a model for the whole country. But we studied the experience in Caxias do Sul because it's more similar to our situation, in terms of size, social makeup and so on.

Do you have the same list of priorities for people to choose from – education, health, paving, sanitation, etc. – as they do in Porto Alegre?

No, we don't provide a list; people come up with their own. In that sense our process is more open than in Porto Alegre. If people decide landscape gardening is the priority, then we'll do what they say. So then the administration has to come before the assembly and argue its own case. We were defeated in several regional assemblies from the very first year. For example, we would come forward with all the technical arguments to explain why the priority had to be education, but no, people voted for health.

We made some changes too, after the first year, because the PB is always under construction. Before, for example, once the assemblies in the regions and subregions had decided their priorities, it was the PB councillors, those elected from the assemblies, who went away and decided in the PB council how the resources should be divided among different regions and their priorities, and which schools, health centres, roads or whatever should be built where. But we discovered that people on the ground were complaining they never found out exactly how the money was spent. We saw there was a real danger of the PB councillors losing touch with the people who'd elected them. So now the councillors decide on how the resources should be shared out, but it goes back to the regional assemblies to decide exactly which pipes, paving stones or football pitches should be put in where, using those resources. In this way we strengthened further the element of direct democracy.

The participatory budget council still has the important task of supervising the financing and execution of those works. Some of the other local governments where other versions of the participatory budget have been applied argue that people are too prone to vote only as a function of their own immediate neighbourhood's interests. They say that broader projects, which are of interest to the wider community, don't get a look in. So they argue that these bigger projects should be kept out of the PB and decided by the city hall administration. My position is that the city hall has to go into those regional assemblies and argue the case for the works of more general interest. You cannot start from the assumption that people have corporatist instincts, and will only see the immediate interests of their own neighbourhood. If that happens it's because we aren't politicising the debate enough.

What we did find was that it was necessary to set up some additional thematic assemblies to discuss particular areas that it's difficult to address adequately in the ordinary regional assemblies. So for the 2002/03 participatory budget we introduced assemblies dealing specifically with the needs of women, black people, the disabled and youth, as well as one devoted specifically to urban development, which could deal more adequately with environmental questions for example. Each of these now votes on one priority policy for their area. In fact there is a fine dividing line between being thoroughly radical about extending and deepening the process of direct democracy in the regional assemblies on the one hand, and on the other applying more 'liberal' notions of setting aside space for 'minority' interests – or interests that are still, I would argue, politically minority issues because they haven't yet been taken on board by the majority of the population. The environment is an example. In the first year, out of all eight regions and 25 subregions, in only one case was the environment selected as one of the three priorities. And that was in spite of us at city hall arguing in favour. Of course it's a question of political maturity.

Anyway, the PB council decided that 20 per cent of the budget would be set aside for the priorities of these new thematic assemblies, while the other 80 per cent would go to the regional assemblies. This was a proposal we took into the PB council and argued for, and people agreed.

So it's a process and we're learning. But the fact that our model of PB has decisionmaking powers means we're expanding the democratic space. When we said that from the first year we would open 100 per cent of our investments to a PB with decisionmaking powers, and that we'd leave it to the assemblies to come up with their own lists of priorities to choose from, some other administrations criticised us heavily. People said we were mad. They asked how we expected to fulfil our election promises. I said, well, we'll have to go into those plenary sessions and defend our proposals. As a local government we mustn't be afraid of direct democracy. And of course we often lost that first year, and we've often lost since then. I went just the other day to one of the assemblies – we *know* the region needs a creche, I went with all the figures, but the assembly voted in favour of paving the road! So they won't get their creche. Will the mothers complain? Yes they certainly will. What can we say? Only that it's the PB that decides, and you'll have go back into that assembly next year and argue for it. It's an educational process too.

I got it in the neck in one neighbourhood. The majority of the population only took part in some of their local assembly. So it was a particular minority that got to decide which streets would be the priority. The others went to the press and accused me of being responsible. So what could I say? Simple. Next year you make sure *you* take part and decide. That's the way people learn. In fact they were right. The other streets were much more of a priority, that's where the asphalting should have begun. But they didn't go to the plenaries, and they didn't argue their case. If I back down, accept their argument and override the PB, even in the case of one single street, then I undermine the entire participatory budget. So it's a permanent political battle.

Do you think there are clear differences between a revolutionary way of implementing the participatory budget and a reformist way of doing it?

There certainly are. If you want to apply it in a reformist way, using a social democratic approach, then the participatory budget is in fact easier to apply than in a revolutionary way.

How so?

If you have consultative assemblies, if you create mechanisms for indirect representation, and hold discussions of this and that in forums, then you *are* mobilising the population. But you're not actually building a power structure. When the PB is revolutionary, that's what it's doing. It's beginning to build a power structure – an autonomous power structure within the society. From a theoretical point of view what you're doing is building structures of control within the state apparatus, whereby civil society begins to exert control over the state. It begins to expose and eliminate, or at least redress, the endemic corruption. It oversees public works and breaks down the cosy relationship between public administration and private contractors. It demystifies the notion that the budget is something technical, fixed in stone, out of reach, and shows it to be something very basic. It's about what money comes in and where it goes. And that is something that people can control and supervise, month after month. That's a revolutionary proposal.

But when you hold consultative forums so you can say you are listening to people, you're not opening up spaces for them to exercise power or creating new forms of power. In fact the PB is no longer just a banner of the PT. There are even local governments of the right-wing Liberal Front Party (PFL)[2] applying their own version of the PB. From the neoliberal point of view, the PB looks very 'modern'. And some PT administrations also apply similar 'consultative' versions of the PB, which are very different from the revolutionary proposal.

So the model of participatory budget you choose is absolutely fundamental.

So are you saying that a participatory budget with decisionmaking powers is incompatible with a reformist approach?

Yes it's incompatible. A budget is the expression of a government's priorities. It's the expression of the economic class that dominates the state apparatus. That's the same whether it's the state at municipal, state or national level. As soon as you create the space for the majority of society to control this instrument, it becomes incompatible with any right-wing project, because the working classes and other sectors that are excluded from power will begin to express their class interests and not those of the capitalist class.

So when the World Bank and the UN praise the participatory budget as an example of transparent, efficient local administration...

They don't understand. Not that they're being ingenuous; but when the model is a decisionmaking one, and when the state structures stimulate the popular classes to exercise that power, they don't grasp the significance of that. When you organise forums and debates, invite civil society to spend two days discussing housing, two days discussing health and education, and hear what they have to say, that's something the World Bank can praise. That's all very nice. But it's different if you create a power structure, where people discuss income and expenditure and decide the investments. That's incompatible.

But the power of local government is very limited. It exists within a space shaped by others. So this decisionmaking power is still very restricted.

But people don't actually live in 'states' or even 'countries'. State and nation are the fictions of government bureaucracy. People live in cities or towns or regions, where they can begin to learn, as part of an educational process, that power is something they can begin to exercise themselves.

But many things that determine people's lives here in Araraquara don't pass through the hands of local government.

In every regional assembly these things come up – the tax system, paying the foreign debt...

Exactly. The city hall in Araraquara doesn't decide whether or not to pay the foreign debt.

But it politicises society. The important thing is not how much we decide locally. It's that we're educating people and showing them that they can organise themselves to exercise power. If every municipality did this you'd have a network of popular organisation in each city, town and area that would create a very different structure of power. That's really what we're investing in. We're investing in popular organisation, in another kind of political power.

That all sounds great. But it seems the revolutionary left in the PT often does this without making any reference to fundamental social change, to socialism in fact.

I don't think you can turn up at a public assembly where people have never heard of socialism, or only heard a distorted version of it, and start expounding in favour of socialism. What you can do is begin to show people what power structures in a socialist society might look like, based on democracy. So we're not just talking to people about it, we're *showing* them.

Maybe this innovation means more in a country of the South, like Brazil. In the North, in Europe for example, there have been quite a few experiences of 'municipal socialism' under Labour or Social Democratic parties, with public participation in running schools and other social services, or like the city councils run by Communist parties in places like Bologna. But these have never really challenged the overall structures of power. So isn't there a danger, even with the approach you've outlined, that all this remains an interesting oasis in a wider world that doesn't change?

That might be true if we were talking about an isolated political experience. But that's not what I see. Even allowing for the different approaches that exist, I see the PB as something much wider. We had a forum here in Araraquara where we brought together more than 50 municipalities from São Paulo state alone, with all the main political leaders from the PT and other parties. So I think we're talking about a project that, although still ambiguous because the model is in dispute, is no longer isolated. It is growing and is seen as important by very broad sections of society. Within this, the battle over the model between revolutionary and reformist versions of the participatory budget is something we have to keep pushing forward.

Let me suggest a different alternative. In Argentina, after December 2001, there was a rapid growth of popular assemblies. The left in different parts of the world begin to describe it as a kind of Paris Commune, as popular power from the bottom up. That seemed to be a very different way of building an alternative structure of power, outside the existing state. And it seemed to many on the left to be much closer to traditional views of what popular power might look like. The PB, however, is rather more inside the existing state, or half inside and half outside.

Let's be clear. The PB is not a structure to legitimate the existing state, like the organs of so-called popular power were in Eastern

Europe. The PB must be *autonomous* from the state. But it's not 'autonomist' in the libertarian or anarchist sense. The structures of the PB require a vanguard to organise them, encourage them, push them forward, all the while understanding that they must be autonomous. Why is it important for us win local elections? It's not just to show that the left can be good administrators. It is also – and this is what I always tell people at city hall – because what will remain when we're gone is popular organisation. We have to stimulate this organisation of the people and create a different power structure that can fight over the direction society is going in.

Raul Pont has lamented the absence of proposals for workers' control from the trade union movement in Brazil. Of course the classic Marxist tradition sees the productive sector as key. In that sense, isn't the PB's kind of control by the people over the local state, at city level, without any workers' control over production, destined to run aground?

Firstly, a significant part of society, especially in Latin America, is outside the productive sector. It's excluded. And this part of society has just as much revolutionary potential as the traditional working class, perhaps even more. If you look at the landless movement, it's not just agricultural workers; it's the excluded who are fighting for land in Brazil. The same goes for the homeless. It's not the proletariat that's confronting the state; it's people with nowhere to live. So I don't think the subject of history is to be found just within the classic Marxist conception of the working class.

Not just. But surely if you don't take account of the productive sector you won't get very far?

Of course the productive sector is important. It has revolutionary potential. But faced with the present capitalist offensive, it's a sector that's very much on the defensive, in retreat, which finds it very difficult to take any political initiatives. Today in Latin America it's not the working class that is taking political initiatives, questioning the economic model, or challenging capitalism.

But here in Araraquara, do you see any ways of encouraging workers in production to take such initiatives?

As a matter of fact, our big debate in the PT with the trade unions has been that they want some areas of investment to be discussed specifically with them. What we've said to them is, go along to the PB assemblies and argue for your positions there. There is no reason why the trade unions should have a privileged position. They should organise to go into the PB and win their arguments there. Otherwise we fall into a logic where some sections of society are more important than others. And if we follow that logic we'll fall into exactly the kinds of mistakes made in Eastern Europe.

But, to take one example, city hall has absolutely no control over whether or not a big factory like the aircraft manufacturer Embraer moves to Araraquara.[3]

But the people of this municipality *can* discuss and decide whether or not we should spend any money on Embraer setting up here. If there's any suggestion of city hall's putting public money into bringing Embraer here, then that has to go to the PB.

But surely what the PB discusses is still limited to the distribution of society's wealth. What it cannot discuss is the actual production of that wealth.

But it can. If you look at the PB regional assemblies in Araraquara you'll find that four out of the eight regions have decided to prioritise policies to generate jobs and income.

But in the end in a capitalist economy it's those who own and control the capital that decide what gets produced and how.

Of course. The participatory budget certainly does not overcome class contradictions. The participatory budget creates a power structure. It develops people's collective strength, so that at some point, if this structure grows, you will bring the existing class structure into question. But to say that the PB itself challenges the class structure is wrong. That would be to ask something of the PB that is beyond its scope.

Workers' control over production is clearly something more ambitious than just conventional trade unionism. It means workers beginning to have a say over what is produced and how, which in the end decides much of the shape of society. Surely the PB won't take you that far, right?

You must remember that the PB is permanently under construction. The models are changing and being developed all the time. What's important is the kind of PB you're building. If it has the power to decide, if it's a revolutionary model, then it's certainly going to create an alternative power structure within the state. At some point it may become necessary for the structures of popular participation to begin discussing the system of production. This implies a good deal of political education for those taking part. They're certainly getting that here in Araraquara. But there's a whole level of class consciousness to be built up before it's clear to everyone that it's not enough to discuss the result of what's produced, that production itself has to be discussed as well.

However, for the time being we have a more pressing concern. As a local government that sees itself as a kind of revolutionary vanguard, giving a lead in helping to build an autonomous form of popular participation, we have to be constantly on guard against the process turning in upon itself and becoming ossified.

This is a real danger. Still, I'm confident that we're building a kind of participatory budget that *is* revolutionary, that *is* developing a new structure of power. It's a process of accumulation. How far that accumulation goes, and how far it leads to new initiatives, I can't say. I can't give you a time scale. But I'm sure it's leading in that direction.

THE EXPERIENCE IN CAXIAS DO SUL

Pepe Vargas[4]

When we were first elected in 1996, our basic idea was the same as in Porto Alegre – to go beyond classic liberal democracy, to overcome the distance between governors and governed, to try to go beyond citizens being passive objects of policy and have them become active subjects of political decisionmaking, and to build a new kind of democracy.

However, although the main mechanisms are the same, a number of differences soon developed. This was not a deliberate attempt by us to 'correct the weaknesses' of Porto Alegre. Rather it was a product of our determination not to impose or transplant something from outside, but to invite the population to discuss and decide the form of its own participatory budget. The differences therefore come from the people themselves. They reflect the different realities of the two cities and the different histories of their social movements.

For example people began to see there was a danger of geographical bias in the election of PB delegates. Our regions are spread over quite large areas. That means that, when it comes to the regional assemblies, it's a lot easier for people from the neighbourhoods closest to the venue to attend in large numbers. As a result they could get more delegates than the neighbourhoods further away, and have an unfair advantage when it comes to deciding the allocation of investments. So we introduced a compensatory mechanism, whereby the turnout at more local, subregional meetings is taken into account to 'make up' the numbers for neighbourhoods that may have been under-represented at the main regional assemblies. There are several similar differences in our mechanisms.

There has also been a difference in people's priorities. When we took office the health facilities in Caxias do Sul were very poor. So in the early years health always came out as people's first priority. Now the health issues have largely been dealt with. Indeed few cities in Brazil have a health service that matches ours today. So now the main priority is paving the streets. That's almost the exact opposite of how the PB priorities developed in Porto Alegre.

From participatory budget to participatory planning

We are now concentrating on finding ways of integrating the participatory budget – based on the nine city regions plus a tenth region taking in rural areas around the city – with longer-term planning for the municipality as a whole.

This is a natural progression. Although people start with very local demands – relating to their street, neighbourhood or region – they gradually move on to develop an understanding of the needs of the city as a whole. As they gain access to the numbers of the public budget and decide its priorities, they begin to become planners of the city they want to build for themselves and those close to them. They lay the basis for moving beyond vertical, technocratic planning towards a horizontal, democratic form of planning.

Obviously local government plays an important part in this. It has to share information, organise the planning process, use its technical and political staff to analyse the problems and formulate proposals, in permanent dialogue with the community's own knowledge and expertise. This means understanding that in this process all of us – on the local government side as well as on the community side – are both educators and educated.[5] It means understanding that we are breaking with the traditionally authoritarian idea of planning that gives primacy to experts, imposing their priorities from the top down ('technocratic vertical planning'). Instead we are asserting a new idea of 'democratic horizontal planning', in which technical expertise is indispensable but goes hand in hand with the knowledge of the people, in a dialectical relationship.

From theory to practice

One thing we've had to confront is the kind of centralisation that has marked the entire history of Caxias do Sul, ever since it was founded in 1875 as part of a project for settling Italian immigrants in southern Brazil. This meant that the legal framework regulating the way the city's land was occupied and used, the policies directing its investments, and the organisation of its road and transport systems all revolved around the historic centre.

Over time this merely accentuated the general pattern of urban development in Brazil: large chunks of the population are pushed into the margins and the city is split between top-class facilities for the few and a total absence of infrastructure for the many. More recently, however, even the historic centre has lost much of its economic and social vitality. The priority given to commerce and business has driven away residents and produced an impoverished, lifeless public space, increasingly occupied by some of the poorest sections of the population, while the rich retire into the private spaces of the shopping malls, social clubs and closed condominiums. This dynamic and the chaotic growth of the city have also put pressure on the surrounding rural areas.

Even before we were elected, in 1996, a group of urban planners from the previous administration's Municipal Planning Cabinet (as it happens they were all members of our party, the Workers' Party) proposed a new set of guidelines for the city's development. They succeeded in getting these debated with civil society bodies in a series of public forums, resulting in legislation for a new urban plan. There is not room here to go into all the details of the new system for zoning land use, introducing land occupation rates and building limits and a series of other norms established in this law. The main idea however was to decentralise the city. The city was divided into nine sectors or regions, with building limits set at an attractive level in the centre of each of these regions. The aim was to offer in these regional centres the kinds of services and activities that had only been available in the historic centre, either through private investment or public sector intervention, thus democratising commercial opportunities and increasing social mobility. Combined with strict limits on building beyond the city perimeter, these measures in the new urban plan also aimed to reduce pressure on the rural area and preserve its environment.

When we began to introduce the participatory budget in Caxias do Sul, from 1997 onwards, we decided to use these nine planning sectors as the basis for organising the regional PB assemblies. Local neighbourhood associations helped draw up the boundaries on the basis of the city's strong tradition of community organisation. In the case of the tenth, rural region, which takes in all the rural areas around the city and accounts for 7.5 per cent of the total population of 376,000 inhabitants, the agricultural workers' union took on that role.

This combination of the urban plan and the PB, based on the same geographical units, aimed to bring together local demands, by street and neighbourhood, with a broader dimension, that of the region as a whole. We are now looking to deepen this combination by subdividing both the PB regions and the urban plan sectors into common territorial planning units. These would be something like micro-regions, and would aim to deepen the degree of popular participation in the territorial planning process.

The main weakness of this system of deciding investments on a regional basis is that it makes it difficult to discuss sectoral policies and big works for the whole city. A typical example is the problem we have had in not spending enough on housing, once the population had prioritised health, education, sanitation and paving.

So far the demands and priorities at the level of the city as a whole – what we call the 'macro-guidelines' – have been something for us in the city hall administration to present to the participatory budget council, made up of PB councillors elected from the regional assemblies. Of course we then have to win the argument in the PB council, which can and does change our proposals if it sees fit. So that is already an important democratic advance. But we want the macro-guidelines to be debated by every citizen in his or her neighbourhood. That is what our proposal for participatory planning aims to achieve.

This is still at an initial stage. We're beginning pilot schemes to bring together a wide range of social movements, community organisations and pressure groups of one sort or another to discuss with us some of the medium and long-term priorities – things like the city's public spaces, where they should be located and what they should be used for. The idea is not to bypass the participatory budget but to enrich it by providing a whole new set of inputs. When people go along to their PB assembly they should already have the information and issues at their fingertips, to be able to debate and decide these longer-term, broader issues. Then instead of the PB council deciding whether or not to put aside money from this year's investments for longer-term projects, the citizens themselves can collectively make these decisions.

We're also introducing four thematic assemblies, like those in Porto Alegre, where all citizens who are interested can come along to debate and decide the macro-guidelines for four specific sectors: social inclusion, economic development, urban development, and culture, sport and leisure. These assemblies will then present their conclusions to the PB council.

As a result of these developments in the PB, it will no longer be local government and its technicians that shape the broader debate over planning the city's future, but the population as a whole. In all these areas local government will seek to encourage discussion of cross-sectoral policies to overcome inequalities of gender, race, age and sexual orientation.

Of course, even when integrated into a dynamic of municipal planning, as here, the participatory budget is not itself an instrument of social change. Only a much deeper transformation can resolve the contradiction between the PB and prevailing inequalities and injustice. However, the PB does distribute resources better and apply them more efficiently. And it does address one issue that is central to overcoming these inequalities – the question of democracy. In fact it radicalises democracy. This question of radicalising democracy is not a tactical one for us; it's a strategic one. It's a fundamental part of where we want to get to, of the kind of socialism we want. So in so far as the PB radicalises democracy, we are already engaging with a central feature of our longer-term goal.

6
On a Bigger Scale: Rio Grande do Sul and Nationwide

Ubiratan de Souza

In 1998, after almost a decade in office in Porto Alegre, the Workers' Party (PT) won the elections for governor of Rio Grande do Sul state. Olívio Dutra, who had been the first PT mayor of the city, became the first PT governor of the state. Many believed it would prove impossible to transfer the experience of Porto Alegre's participatory budget to state level. Not only was the scale of the task so much larger. The undemocratic traditions of Brazilian political life – the networks of patronage, nepotism and corruption – were much more deeply entrenched in many of the small towns and rural areas that made up most of this state of just over 10 million inhabitants. The election campaign itself had been deeply polarised; with just 50.78 per cent against 49.22 per cent in the second round, the PT's victory was by the smallest of margins. Yet despite intense opposition from conservative interests in the state, the Rio Grande do Sul participatory budget was widely regarded as a success. In this chapter Ubiratan de Souza considers some of the specific features of the state-level PB in Rio Grande do Sul and how they could be developed in a federal-level participatory budget for the whole of Brazil.

The success in implementing the PB at state level, during the administration of Olívio Dutra as governor of Rio Grande do Sul state (1998–2002), has debunked the argument of those on the right in favour of centralised control that the PB was only possible at town or city level. They claimed that the PB could not be applied at state or national level because these levels were economically and politically too complex. In fact the contrary was the case. Putting it into practice on a larger scale – the state of Rio Grande do Sul covers 282 square kilometres, includes 497 municipalities and a population of around 10 million – hugely increased the financial resources potentially available, both from within the budget itself and from external sources. The existence of a publicly owned state bank, BARISUL, as well as access to credit from the national development bank, BNDES, and the Bank of Brazil, meant that significant resources were available to finance some of the central projects discussed within the Rio Grande do Sul participatory budget, in the areas of agriculture, employment and income generation, and regional economic development.

The larger scale also gave the PB increased legal powers to influence social policies affecting the whole state. These policies included: transport (paving state highways linking various towns, bridge building, etc.); housing (rural housing, cooperatives, giving deeds to land squats, low-cost housing, etc.); environment and sanitation; crime prevention; education (the state network of primary and middle schools, creation of a state university, etc.); health (setting up regional and municipal public health programmes); agriculture (land reform, family farms, anti-poverty programmes in the countryside, etc.), employment and income generation (first job programmes, support for medium, small and micro-businesses, a people's economy of cooperation and solidarity, support for systems of local production, etc.); energy (lighting in rural areas, expansion of electricity generation and distribution, etc.); social inclusion (minimum income and citizenship networks) and regional economic development.

BETTER STATE–MUNICIPAL RELATIONS

Unlike the PB in Porto Alegre – where local government relates directly to the population – the PB in Rio Grande do Sul means that the state government relates not only to the population directly but also to local administrations.

This opens up the possibility of improving the relationship between these two levels of government through popular participation and control. The discretionary funds available to the state government to spend on public programmes, either directly in regions and municipalities or in partnership with municipal governments, are allocated in accordance with the priorities decided in the state PB and a set of objective criteria. The system works in a very similar way to the system used to determine the distribution of resources in the Porto Alegre PB. Distribution of resources between different regions and municipalities is decided based on a formula reflecting: the regional and thematic priorities chosen through the PB; the total population of the different regions; and the shortfall in services and infrastructure in different areas.

Given the bigger geographical scale and greater complexity of public policies at state level, thematic and sectoral councils take on a more substantial role. Municipal councils for health, social services, agriculture, housing, and so on, alongside the PB delegates, play a key part in both drawing up and implementing the budget. They oversee the projects carried out directly by the state government as well as those done in partnership with municipal governments.

Traditional political relations, heavily marked by patronage, favouritism and corruption, have begun to give way to a new form of public administration controlled by the population and directed towards combating regional inequalities. As a result, the federal pact between state and municipality has been strengthened, and the political culture of the state has begun a profound mutation.

At the same time the state-level PB has created mechanisms of direct democracy and participatory planning that enable citizens in all 497 municipalities across Rio Grande do Sul to take part in decisionmaking PB public assemblies. In these assemblies citizens can debate and assert their wishes in three separate votes. In the first round they vote for three priority themes and programmes in the areas of economic and social development, employment and income generation, and social inclusion. In the second round they vote for three priority themes and demands related to public works and services. In the third they elect their PB delegate from amongst those present at the assembly, on the basis of one delegate for every 20 participants.

Table 6.1   How it works – the participatory budget in Rio Grande do Sul state, 1999–2002

Direct and universal participation of citizens in all 23 regions and 497 municipalities of Rio Grande do Sul, to debate, decide and control the state budget.

It debates and decides the totality of the state budget and state policies. The PB is a system of administration that begins by deciding priorities and goes on to draw up the budget and control its implementation – all of this is done by the population in general and by PB delegates and councillors, through thematic and sectoral councils at regional and municipal levels.

Regional assemblies to decide guidelines. Held in each of the state's 23 regions during March. Open to direct participation by all citizens living in the municipalities making up that region. They debate and decide the guidelines that will be used in the open municipal assemblies to discuss priorities for development programmes, public works and services that affect the state as a whole.

Regional assemblies on development themes. Held at the same times and in the same places as the Regional Guideline Assemblies. They too are open to direct participation by all citizens living in the municipalities making up that region. They debate and begin to decide, in each region, the thematic priorities for development programmes affecting the state as a whole. This decisionmaking process is then continued and concluded in the open municipal assemblies. These regional thematic assemblies also elect delegates (one for every 20 participants) who will represent the region in the regional delegates' assembly.

Open municipal assemblies. Held in the 497 municipalities across the state between 20 March and 31 May. Open to direct participation by all citizens. The population debates and votes on two sets of priorities: first, the order of priorities amongst different kinds of development programmes affecting the whole state; second, the order of priorities amongst different kinds of public works and services demanded in that region. These municipal assemblies also elect delegates (one for every 20 participants) who will represent the municipality's agreed priorities within the regional delegates' assembly.

Regional delegates' assemblies. Held in each of the state's 23 regions at the end of June and again at the beginning of September. Delegates from the municipal assemblies and the thematic assemblies take part. These delegates are presented with the state government's income projections and the main budget headings for expenditure (wages bill, overheads and related services, investments, debt servicing). They also receive a list of all the statewide development programmes and all the demands for regional public works and services, and the order in which the population in the open assemblies has prioritised these. These delegates' assemblies also elect the councillors who will represent the region on the state PB council, the body that coordinates the entire PB process.

State PB council (CPB) and regional delegates' plenaries. In a series of meetings in the CPB and regional delegates' plenaries in August and September, the councillors and delegates, along with the state government, now try to organise and reconcile the different demands for public works and services in each region and for development programmes affecting the whole state, on the basis of the projected income, the main categories of expenditure and the agreed criteria for distributing resources between the regions (priority themes, population size, index of need for services and infrastructure). Throughout, they have to take account of and respect the order of priorities established by popular vote in the open assemblies. In this way they draw up and decide a proposed budget and plan of investments and services to be carried out by the state government.

This budget proposal is presented to the state legislative assembly by 15 September. The assembly has until 30 November to debate it and approve it.

The budget and plan of investments and services, once approved by the legislative assembly, becomes law and comes into effect the following year from January until 31 December.

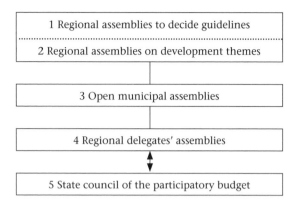

Figure 6.1   Stages of the participatory budget in Rio Grande do Sul

Software was developed that makes it possible to process and publish the results then and there. Later the results are collated across the regions and the state as a whole. They then become the planning indicators used to draw up the detailed budget, along with indicators dealing with the resources needed by the state government to pay for existing pubic services, institutional planning needs and other general charges.

Table 6.2   Facts and figures on the state of Rio Grande do Sul

Population	10.17 million	UN Human Development Index 0.869	
Size	282,000 km^2	Infant mortality	14.9/1000
Municipalities	497	Life	Men	74
GDP	R$ 92,861 billion	Expectancy	Women	79
General budget	R$ 13,245 billion	Illiteracy	7.19%

Source: Brazilian Institue of Geography & Statistics

Table 6.3   The participatory budget in Rio Grande do Sul in numbers

Item	1999	2000	2001	2002
Participants	188,528	281,926	378,340	333,040
Delegates elected	8,460	13,987	18,601	16,145
Open assemblies held	644	670	735	775

Notes:
Open public assemblies: The PB held a total of 2,824 public assemblies in Rio Grande do Sul between 1999 and 2002.
Participants: The PB brought together, in its four years, a total of 1.2 million citizens.

Source: Budget and Finance Cabinet and Community Relations Cabinet, Government of the state of Rio Grande do Sul

Table 6.4   Rio Grande do Sul priorities selected by the population in the participatory budget process

	1999/00	2000/01	2001/02	2002/03
Works and services				
1st place	Agriculture	Education	Education	Education
2nd place	Education	Agriculture	Health	Health
3rd place	Health	Transport	Transport	Transport
Development themes				
1st place	Agriculture	Agriculture	Education	Agriculture
2nd place	Employment and income generation	State university	Agriculture	Employment and income generation
3rd place	Transport	Transport	Employment and income generation	Education

Source: Budget and Finance Cabinet, Government of the state of Rio Grande do Sul

CAN THE PARTICIPATORY BUDGET WORK AT NATIONAL LEVEL?

There is absolutely no reason why the participatory budget should not be applied at national or federal level, for the whole of Brazil. On the basis of the experience already acquired, we can lay out some of the main aspects.

As far as feasibility goes, a participatory budget across Brazil should in fact be easier, because its legal powers to implement policies of social and economic development would be greater, and so would the financial resources available. Of course, such policies at national level are inevitably more complicated. Therefore, in addition to the direct participation of citizens deciding priority areas and programmes in the assemblies of the national PB, it would also be necessary to give a substantial role to the social movements and to the sectoral and thematic councils in formulating these programmes and overseeing their implementation.

Given the budget allocations for investments and related services, as well as the credit available from the National Development Bank, the Bank of Brazil and the Federal Savings Bank, there should be no problem drawing up a list of the kinds of social and economic development programmes and public works and services that could be discussed and decided by the whole population of Brazil in the Brazilian participatory budget. These programmes would have to meet the technical and legal criteria that would allow them to be implemented either directly by the federal government or in partnership with the state and municipal governments, under the control of PB delegates and the various thematic and sectoral councils.

In this national-level PB, we would have, in addition to a direct relationship with the population, other political agents like the state and municipal administrations. This should strengthen the federal pact. It would allow the federal government's own funding for development policies, public works and services, as well as those it carries out in partnership with local and regional governments, to be submitted to the scrutiny of popular participation in the participatory budget. At the same time they would be subject to the PB's objective criteria for a fairer redistribution of resources, in order to even out imbalances between different regions of the country.

Another key question would be guaranteeing direct participation by citizens across Brazil, in every state, region and municipality, in public PB assemblies with full decisionmaking powers. We already have the methodology of direct democracy and participatory planning to do this. We also have the software to collect and collate the priorities decided by the population, which we used at state level in Rio Grande do Sul. These can be the starting point for a Brazil-wide participatory budget. There is no perfect blueprint for this. The national PB, like those that have gone before it, will be an open, dialectical, learning process. Together, citizens, social movements, the thematic and sectoral councils and the government itself will continuously create new and varied mechanisms for direct democracy and participatory planning. There would still be the question of how to organise and mobilise people for these public assemblies. In coordination with the federal government, the social movements and other organisations of civil society, as well as states and municipalities, would take responsibility for publicising and mobilising for and organising the infrastructure of these assemblies. This would give the national PB greater autonomy from the state from the outset. We had a very positive experience of this in the Rio Grande do Sul participatory budget, during the period when a ruling by the conservative-controlled judiciary prohibited the state government from providing any support or infrastructure for PB public assemblies. In response, the PB delegates, local mayors, popular organisations and the population in general took over the work of organising the meetings in an impressive show of self-organisation.

This episode showed how the PB process is more than just an exercise in extending democratic public control and planning. It is also a political process generating awareness and citizenship.

The struggle against social exclusion demands public policies that shift the distribution of wealth in this country, at the same time as they implement different forms of direct participation by the population in managing public affairs.

Participatory democracy was a central part of the guidelines for a governmental programme agreed by the Workers' Party (PT) at its conference in 2001.[1] However, this approach to democracy was watered down in the government programme put forward by Lula and the PT's leaders at the beginning of the presidential election campaign in July 2002. The idea wasn't rejected, but it wasn't given the prominence it had before.

In the first year of Lula's presidency, there were some limited moves in this direction. A series of public debates were held to discuss the government's multi-year plan. Some ministries began to involve social movements and sectors of civil society in formulating future policy. This was certainly an advance in comparison with the previous government. But it fell well short of what is needed, if we are to avoid squandering the enormous energy and enthusiasm that Lula's victory unleashed amongst millions of Brazilian citizens.

An open, direct debate with the Brazilian people over the federal budget – a national participatory budget – is one of the key steps for advancing a democratic revolution in the country and developing an alternative model of development. When you open up the black box of the federal budget you begin to understand the relation between the state and society, and the political choices available in terms of fair taxation and spending. You see how most of the budget is committed to paying interest and capital on the public debt, severely restricting what is available for social spending. You grasp the implications of guaranteeing respect for the budget surplus targets contained in Brazil's agreement with the International Monetary Fund.[2]

President Lula has used one of his characteristic football metaphors to say that 'the people should not remain in the stands as spectators, but get out on the pitch and play along with the government.' This is right. Our project, the PT's project, can only move forward if the social movements and citizens in general mobilise – to support the government, but also to *push* the government into the big struggles needed to change our country.

The demand for a nationwide participatory budget is now a fundamental part of the struggle to change the direction taken by our PT government.

Part III

What it Means

7

Participatory Democracy and Local Power: The Experience of Porto Alegre[1]

Raul Pont[2]

If we want to analyse the experience of participatory democracy in Porto Alegre, it's important to remember that although the proposal was contained in the party programme with which we won the local government elections in 1988, it was still a very vague idea. In Brazil there had never been any concrete examples that could serve as models for this sort of popular participation and democracy. We had made a commitment, and we had the political will, to go beyond representative democracy. But we knew this would be a learning process, in which the participants, the citizens of Porto Alegre, would have to play an active part alongside us in making it happen.

We were also well aware of the limitations of such a local experiment in a country where political power is so highly centralised. Nonetheless, we were convinced that from a tactical point of view (in terms of democratisation, transparency and administrative efficiency) and from a strategic one too (in terms of inversion of priorities, a new relation between state and society, and the predominance of new social actors), our government absolutely needed to develop participatory democracy. The existence of a legal basis, as well as the legitimacy coming from our victory at the polls, gave us the courage to seek out that popular participation.

The Brazilian Constitution adopted in 1988[3] had stated in its first article, 'All power emanates from the people, who exercise it through elected representatives, or directly, according to the terms of this Constitution.' The new charter thus incorporated the idea of the direct exercise of popular sovereignty for the first time in Brazil.

It also repeated the classic formulation of modern states that 'all power emanates from the people'. This concept has been present in theory throughout Brazil's republican history but almost always absent from the country's real political practice, marked as it was throughout the last century by exclusionary, oligarchic governments and long periods of dictatorial military rule.

The fact that the Brazilian state contains this contradiction – between the theory of modern constitutional states, with an even more advanced reference to the direct exercise of popular sovereignty, and a very undemocratic reality – is not much different to the situation in other parts of the world.

The liberals who dominated the world's first constitutional regimes never showed much interest in winning social rights. The property qualifications limiting the size of the electorate, the fact that women did not have the right to vote, and a number of implicit and explicit obstacles and prohibitions placed in the way of anti-capitalist parties always gave the liberal political regimes an oligarchic and elitist character.

In Brazil as elsewhere, this was aggravated by a culture of four centuries of plantation slavery, by patronage and paternalism, by the denial of labour rights and long periods of dictatorship. The development of democratic struggles and achievements was never a straightforward process, therefore. It was always marked by conflict and contradiction, even back at its liberal origins.

The 'egalitarian' ideas of Jean-Jacques Rousseau expressed different social interests to the 'possessive', 'property-owning' ideas of John Locke, for example, and led to very different tendencies in the emergence of the capitalist state. Although both began from natural law, which was the basis of liberal thought, for Rousseau the idea of liberty was inseparable from equality as a human condition. Locke's 'possessive individualist' conception, on the other hand, held that the right to liberty was one of the foundations of the right to property, and that it was the job of the state to defend property through the supreme power of parliament.

The point here is not to indulge in a theoretical detour, but to put the origins of the debate about the delegation of power in context. We need to understand that it is not a new debate, and that the different theoretical and ideological explanations have expressed distinct social interests throughout this history. Even today they have different consequences for humankind's political future.

A more radical reading of Brazil's 1988 constitution, in which 'power emanates from the people', involves taking up Rousseau's argument that prior to the act in which the contract of political society is made and a government is agreed upon, there is another moment in which 'the people are the people'. This moment is the primary agreement, the original sovereignty, which cannot be shared, transferred or delegated to the later one.

While this idea bore little relation to the reality around us, it nonetheless pointed towards the big challenge facing any democratic advance within the liberal framework. How can popular sovereignty be maintained? How can we control and reduce the different forms of delegation, in order to maintain popular sovereignty? This question continues to challenge us today.

The main currents of liberalism led to different kinds of representative political systems, but all were anchored in the vision of 'possessive individualism'. This is the case with parliamentary constitutional monarchies and republics, where delegation through the ballot box to parliament unifies executive and legislative functions. But it is also the case with presidential republics, where the executive and legislature have separate powers and separate elections.

This historical process shows with crystal clarity that liberalism is not and never has been synonymous with democracy. During the nineteenth and twentieth centuries, the right to organise trade unions, to form political parties, to universal suffrage, were hard-won achievements just like the struggles for a shorter working day and better conditions. This sort of social reformism later underpinned the welfare state in Europe and a certain level of labour protection in Brazil during the populist period of the mid twentieth century.

New contradictions and class relations produced new political ideas about the world and the relations between society and the state. Socialist thought, especially in its Marxist version, developed a critique of liberal conceptions. It insisted on the class character of the state and its subordination to the interests that dominate in the sphere of production. It also argued that equality in this state of law is no more than a formal, juridical equality meant to conceal the real social inequalities that exist in society.

Even without developing its conception of a socialist state, Marxist thought sought to interpret concrete experiences like the Paris Commune, and to learn the lessons of a new relation between state and society.

The brief experience of the Paris Commune and the various experiences based on councils or soviets in the early years of the Russian Revolution raised once again the question of representation and delegation of power. They sought to go beyond formal, juridical equality and bridge the gap between political power and the majority of the population that characterised classic regimes of liberal, parliamentary representation.

The councils or soviets, whilst retaining a certain degree of delegation, tried to ensure that the producer or worker could simultaneously play a part as legislator through structures based in workplaces and communities, through local, regional and federal councils.

The soviet experience did not survive the civil war and the bureaucratic authoritarianism that prevailed in the Soviet Union's internal struggles in the 1920s. Little by little centralism, the single party, authoritarianism and bureaucratisation eliminated any possibility of a new, socialist democracy, in spite of the nationalisation of the means of production.

The 'really existing socialism' of Eastern Europe, China and other examples on a smaller scale stifled this debate on the left throughout the twentieth century. Democracy, which is inseparable from socialism, ceased to be a strategic element in the programmes of most communist parties. It became subordinated to the tactical interests of the moment.

The predominance of social democratic parties and liberal bourgeois democratic regimes strengthened the perception of representative democracy as the high point of humanity's political achievements.

In most liberal democracies, however, the representative system is now going through a crisis of legitimacy. This is expressed in abstention, apathy and low levels of political and social involvement. Recently it has been aggravated by the developed capitalist countries' difficulty in sustaining the reforms and advances of the welfare state.

In underdeveloped countries, this legitimacy was always limited, partly because of frequent recourse to dictatorship and authoritarian populism, but mainly because here governments and the system have been totally incapable of addressing the brutal social and regional inequalities afflicting these countries.

The lack of legitimacy is also a result of the increasingly bureaucratic and elitist nature of governments and parliaments, and of electoral systems that distort popular representation by imposing barriers on people's participation and using geographical electoral systems that do not respect the right of minorities to have proportional representation. It is further undermined by the increasingly empty quality of the political programmes put forward, and by the fact that even then those elected do not do what they promised. In Brazil the right of elected politicians to hop from party to party without losing their mandates accentuates this still more.

There is another factor in Latin America, especially in Brazil, which has no parallel in Europe or other metropolitan capitalist countries: rapid population growth and breakneck urbanisation. Thirty years ago Brazil had a population of 90 million. One generation later it has almost doubled, with 170 million people in 2001. Fifty years ago two thirds of the population lived in the countryside. Today 80 per cent live in cities.

This process has profoundly changed the country's political landscape. The struggle for access to the basic services that millions of people need to survive in the cities (roads, sewage, healthcare, education, housing) has changed people's behaviour and radically altered the role of local government and the demands placed upon it.

Yet over the last 15 years Brazil's central government has moved in precisely the opposite direction to what social reality requires of it. Neoliberal theory and practice indicated that the way out of underdevelopment was to roll back the state's social functions, privatise essential public services, open up to foreign trade in the most submissive way and allow remittance of profits and debt payments to big international companies and banks. This has meant favouring financial speculation and laying off massive numbers of workers. In other words, there has been a growing disregard for the population's most basic needs.

Not surprisingly, people began to participate more and demand more of their local governments. These began to bear a heavier burden, taking responsibility for more public services without any corresponding changes in the distribution of the country's tax revenue. At present just 14 per cent of all tax receipts in Brazil remain with the municipal administrations, whilst 63 per cent are in the hands of the federal government. The other 23 per cent of the fiscal cake goes to the state governments, which are also responsible for education, health and policing.

In this context we can begin to understand the meaning and importance of our twelve-year experience with participatory democracy in Porto Alegre. We were conscious of the limitations of local actions. We were aware of the need to incorporate them into a larger project – one that would see the country as part of a new conception of the world. But we could not just cross our arms and wait for all the theoretical and strategic problems of the socialist movement to be resolved before taking action at municipal level.

Working together, local government and popular movement, we have built up a rich experience of participation, against the current of neoliberalism. The victory of the PT and its Popular Front electoral alliance in 1988 was a result of the party's growth and the struggles of the social movements throughout that decade. It rested on a programme committed to the real interests of the working classes and it led us to establish new priorities for local government. The most important aspect of this, for us, was that popular participation led to a reversal of priorities.

The best way of ensuring that public resources are spent and invested in line with the public's needs is to change fundamentally the decisionmaking processes. The participatory budget, organised through regional and thematic meetings with open, direct participation and decisionmaking powers, became the key element in a series of measures encouraging citizens to exert direct control over their local government. The municipal councils were consultative bodies covering different sectors of the city's life, which had almost entirely ceased to function. These too became transformed into important forums for discussing and deciding public policies.[4]

Throughout the last twelve years – and now with another mandate beginning for the PT and its allies[5] – a real revolution has occurred in public spending. As a result of increasing popular participation – from fewer than 1,000 people taking part in the first year to 20,000 in the last two years – municipal spending and investment have been redirected towards the priorities decided by the population. Nothing illustrates this better than a comparison between spending on health, social assistance and housing in the first and last years of that period.

In 1989–90, R$91 million, at current values, was spent on these areas (23 per cent of the budget). In 1999–2000 this went up to more than R$360 million (37 per cent of the budget). That's a fourfold increase in social spending between the beginning and end of the decade. Popular involvement and decisionmaking were fundamental in bringing about this growth, which was greater than the growth of the budget itself. But the budget more than doubled over the same period as a result of eliminating tax breaks and incentives and introducing a new code based on progressive taxes and social justice.

The municipal councils mobilised to change public policies in a number of areas, like children and youth, healthcare and education. They achieved both qualitative and quantitative changes in facilities and in the partnerships agreed with community organisations. For example, halfway through our second term we still had very few programmes with community groups working with children and adolescents. Today more than 160 community bodies are receiving public money for creches and a variety of support services, serving thousands of children and young people, all as a result of decisions taken by the population. The same can be said of health facilities or the municipal education system, which has made Porto Alegre the state capital with the highest literacy rate in Brazil.

What experience has taught us over the last twelve years is that the question of democracy is key in any confrontation with neoliberalism. Because of its capacity to mobilise and enlighten, participatory democracy allows people to understand the state and begin to control it; and it serves as a practical demonstration for other political struggles to come.

This experience points again to the limitations of the representative system and the importance of taking up the challenge once more of building participatory democracy, reducing the levels of delegation and bureaucratisation that set in with a merely representative system. That's why the participatory budget has a number of characteristics that have become important points of reference.

The first of these is direct, universal, popular participation through the thematic and regional structures into which the city has been divided. Another is direct action, that is the direct exercise of citizenship – coming together to discuss, learn and decide collectively, to organise meetings and prioritise demands. The third is popular self-organisation, the idea that people's spontaneity, creativity and participation should not be limited by or subordinated to laws voted in the municipal assembly.

We defend this principle against those conservative councillors and deputies who have even resorted to the courts to try to condemn the process as illegal and contrary to representative traditions. They do not accept the population's creating its own rules for its own participation, which can be changed whenever the participants see fit.

The participatory budget's own internal regulations have been developed and improved over these twelve years. They show that by participating and deciding the population can produce rules that are fairer and more objective and show greater solidarity with the poor. The result is a much more democratic way of determining public spending.

In today's world the underdeveloped countries are losing more and more of their national sovereignty. Big international bodies like the World Trade Organisation, the International Monetary Fund and the World Bank are instruments of imperialist corporations and government technocrats. Over these the people exercise neither vote nor influence. The sovereignty of the people and of each citizen is limited more and more to the sphere of local and regional power.

Resisting this process by defending and developing experiences based on local and individual sovereignty is a way of strengthening ourselves, promoting democratic struggles and defending the shared material interests of the majority of the population.

This is the tendency in big urban centres that have to deal with millions of inhabitants demanding services and facilities. It has to be done through citizen participation and local and regional control over these services and investments.

Our election victory in Rio Grande do Sul made it possible to extend this experience to the whole state, linking up with 500 municipalities to draw up and decide the state budget and investment plan. We argue on this basis that the participatory budget and other experiences of participatory democracy raise once again humanity's historic debate over democracy. But this time we start from a new threshold. Modern communications and information technologies have opened up huge new possibilities. And for socialists, the question of democracy is now freed from the bureaucratic vice and authoritarian shackles of the Eastern European experiences.

Neoliberalism, because it is exclusionary, exploitative and authoritarian, is incompatible with democracy and popular sovereignty. In Brazil, the provisional measures that the president can decree[6] have turned the national congress into a caricature of the representative system. It merely adds to the loss of national sovereignty and political legitimacy. The participatory democracy that we have built up over these twelve years, and which has just been confirmed for another four-year period by the people's vote in Porto Alegre, is now reproduced in almost 200 municipalities across Brazil.

It certainly doesn't answer all the country's problems. Its municipal and regional scope is a limitation. Nonetheless, the method shows that it is possible to have policies, as we have in Porto Alegre, which combine social inclusion, the fight against unemployment, bimonthly wage increases in line with inflation, maintenance of public services that are democratically controlled and make a surplus, a balanced budget without layoffs, absolute transparency with moral probity and without corruption, and above all a rising level of popular participation in the way the city's public policies are designed and decided.

Our involvement with international local government networks, in international seminars on participatory democracy, and with the World Social Forum have shown us that we are not alone. There are many of us who believe that another world is possible. Let's go out and build it.

8

Theses on Local Government and the Struggle for Socialism[1]

Raul Pont

The first World Social Forum allowed us to share many varied experiences from every continent of people's resistance to the effects of neoliberal globalisation. Porto Alegre became a huge stage where the exchange of ideas and information made us realise that while our struggles may be local and isolated, they resemble and have the same objectives as many others throughout the world.

We came away more convinced than ever that we are not alone. We understood that there is a common denominator to struggles against national and social exploitation, against racial and sexual discrimination, in defence of the environment – criticising a concept of progress based on a productivism that preys upon nature – against unemployment and exclusion, and in defence of children and youth.

This shared identity comes from an understanding that the battle against neoliberal globalisation takes place on many different levels and that we need to find ever-greater unity amongst these different fights, in terms of both their objectives and their impact.

One example involves movements in underdeveloped countries against paying the foreign debt. A few international campaigns centralise this struggle. But their networks of supporters and activists stretch through dozens of countries, and within these countries are multiplied regionally and locally. Together they keep opposition to the debt alive, share information and organise demonstrations.

In a different way, across Latin America and the Caribbean, the São Paulo Forum has been bringing together political parties, groups and movements every year for over a decade, giving them the chance to learn more about each other, exchange information and experience, and agree on motions and joint actions by consensus. The sense of identity, solidarity and confidence that comes with these meetings is an essential part of preparing for future actions and resolutions, and for bringing together the struggles we have in common.

The second World Social Forum should continue this process. We've already seen how much we have in common. Our activities grow stronger through bringing them together and comparing them. Activists nourish each other and discover new ways forward.

Our thematic group[2] has been discussing relations between society and state, in the context of a crisis in the classical institutions of representative democracy.

Here the question of local power becomes especially important. By that I mean the local and regional governments that anti-neoliberal parties and social movements have been winning control of in several countries around the world. Of course there is a big difference between local government victories in European countries, for example, and Latin America. In Europe the legal, social and political framework is much more deeply rooted and local party contests are much more clearly determined by the national political scene – not that this eliminates the importance of local government even in those countries. In Latin America, however, we have been seeing a rich variety of victories in local government by popular democratic forces and social movements (community organisations and indigenous, trade union and youth groups). These experiences go beyond the national political framework dominated by traditional parties.

These experiences, among which Porto Alegre occupies a prominent position, have spread to many other countries and continents. Today there are hundreds of municipal administrations run by political parties, fronts and broader movements, including indigenous communities, that give another meaning to the public policies they implement.

These local governments involve local communities directly in their decisions and put policies into practice that are opposed to neoliberalism.

Our aim in this text is to try and summarise, in a series of theses, the key characteristics of these experiences in Brazil and in various other countries of Latin America, the Caribbean and Europe that we've had the opportunity to visit and follow. We hope this will help the World Social Forum play its part in reflecting on our various social practices and developing ways of going beyond exclusionary, neoliberal capitalist society.

THESIS I

Local and regional governments provide an experience of participatory democracy through a variety of mechanisms (participatory budgets, municipal councils, city congresses, regional and sectoral forums, neighbourhood boards and even parish groups) that challenge the idea that the classical representative system is inevitable or unchangeable.

Direct, participatory democracy and the sovereignty of popular decisionmaking go beyond the classical notion of citizenship, where delegation through the ballot box transfers decisionmaking power to governments, members of parliament and their parties with no guarantee that they will carry out their mandate. In some cases, like the election of George W. Bush in the US and the Argentine elections later in 2001, abstentions and spoiled votes added up to more than half the electorate, showing just how much the system lacks legitimacy. Direct popular participation and sovereignty make a different kind of relationship possible between people and their government. They can raise people's consciousness and thus revive, in a positive way, the old debate about new kinds of relationships between society and the state.

When they gain access to the detailed figures of the public budget and the city's various development plans, when they get the chance to draw them up and change them, and above all when they win the sovereign power to decide directly how public money should be spent, then ordinary individuals go beyond the limits of citizenship set by bourgeois democracy. They take over the public sphere and are prepared to take up and fight for a project of genuine, substantive democracy, with less bureaucracy and the least possible delegation of power.

THESIS II

Democratic issues are more and more clearly a source of contradiction between the neoliberal capitalist state and its people (as seen in authoritarian centralism, governments with the power to legislate by decree, weakened federal arrangements, and increasingly dictatorial powers for capital in the workplace). They have therefore become a key strategic element of any project for the transition to socialism.

Together with the national question, this is the big programmatic challenge for socialists. Both sets of issues have tremendous power to mobilise people. Both are integral parts of the strategic project that we defend. We cannot accept the conservative argument that experiences of participatory democracy are 'illegal' or 'contrary to classical representative democracy'. (This is the argument that conservative members of the state and municipal assemblies use to take legal action against the participatory budget in Porto Alegre and Rio Grande do Sul.) Such experiences of direct and participatory democracy are legal and legitimate according to both the Brazilian constitution and the country's various municipal charters, as well as in terms of modern constitutional theory, whose first principle is that 'power emanates from the people'.

Even in countries where there may be legal obstacles, we should stand up for the idea that sovereignty emanates from the people, and for the legitimacy of attempts to go beyond mere representation. Such attempts should be encouraged, developed and strengthened. The experiences of participatory democracy already gone through in various countries need to be integrated into our theory and programmatic thinking, so that we can move the political struggle on from local government to central government.

THESIS III

Local government experience is essential if we are to develop, encourage and put into practice people's autonomous, self-organised participation. There can be no democratic socialist project without workers' and producers' self-management in their communities and trade unions and other spaces where they come together. In some countries we can see how re-emerging indigenous community bodies are becoming vehicles for organising local government.

These projects' independence from the prevailing representative system is indispensable. The practical political education the population gains as it discusses and decides on public policies and budgets is a fundamental part of self-organisation.

That is why we strongly defend the principle that the procedural rules governing the participatory budget or other forms of participatory democracy should be drawn up by the participants themselves and open to change by them at any time, not dependent on legislation voted through the municipal council chamber or state assembly.

THESIS IV

Population growth and rapid urbanisation, especially in Latin America, mean that municipalities are taking on more and more responsibilities and services that are critical for the majority of the population: housing, sanitation, healthcare, education and social services. These are areas that an all-powerful, central government cannot possibly run. They are services and historic rights that have never been fully achieved and that neoliberal capitalism is now cutting back. In most cases central government simply abandons its responsibilities and local administrations have to pick up the pieces, without receiving any increase in their share of tax receipts.

Our local governments have to prioritise these areas in their plans, but most importantly they have to transfer the power to decide these priorities to the population, always ensuring the independence of initiatives like the participatory budget and municipal councils.

Our challenge is not to evade the responsibilities of local government just because municipalities in Brazil today get only 14 per cent of the country's total tax income. Indeed in other Latin American countries the situation is similar or worse, because they are more centralised, less federal states.

Our battle must be to use these popular demands and the defence of local government's role to fight for a new distribution of the tax cake and a new kind of federation, in which municipal, provincial and state governments have their political and financial independence strengthened.

These objectives are not at odds with any wider strategy for popular and democratic goals. Such a strategy does not depend on a centralising state. In fact, decentralisation, municipal and provincial autonomy and strengthening local and regional government conflict directly with the authoritarian centralism of neoliberalism.

THESIS V

Local governments are also important as a way of building political hegemony, through participatory democracy and by involving the population in organising and developing public services to meet their daily needs. In this way participatory democracy helps us confront the media and economic power, without underestimating them or thinking that popular participation alone is enough.

Clearly private property and several other institutions of the capitalist state, including concessions to national broadcasting networks, cannot be dealt with at municipal level. But a participatory democracy can build up a network of organisations and associations in areas like services, culture, leisure, sport and even manufacturing and trade through small and micro-businesses, a network that reaches thousands of citizens – forming a kind of social vanguard independent of political parties. This is a network of opinion-formers, who will naturally defend the project that made them protagonists of their own day-to-day existence and the policies that they implement together with local government.

If we bring together the hundreds of neighbourhood and trade union bodies, the community associations working with children and adolescents, cultural, religious and sporting bodies, and we build a participatory democracy with them that decides on public policies and budgets – as we have with the participatory budget and municipal councils – then we will be building a powerful network of support for our political project.

This also applies to those areas of responsibility taken on by local government because the neoliberal central government has abandoned them. When we build health, education and social service networks involving democratic participation by service providers, public sector workers also tend to embrace our political project and free themselves from the influence of central government.

THESIS VI

Local governments can also provide a potent example for a whole range of anti-neoliberal policies.

When we put a stop to tax breaks and other fiscal benefits for capitalists, we demonstrate that it is possible to balance the books without resorting to cuts in jobs or services. Similarly, in opposition to the neoliberal right, we can show in practice that we can have well-managed public enterprises capable of generating a surplus for reinvestment. The defence of public utilities in electricity, water, transport and, in the case of state governments, public banks operating on new lines are all concrete ways of confronting the wave of privatisations implemented by our countries' central governments.

When we implement wage increases in line with inflation, when we attack the huge disparities in public-sector pay, when we defend a state pension system run by the state employees themselves, we are also challenging neoliberal ideology. These policies serve as an example for thousands of other workers who see them as justifying their own struggles for similar gains in the private sector and throughout society.

THESIS VII

The electoral victories that have opened the way to such experiences of local government have been achieved in Latin America by fronts of left-wing political parties or by fronts of urban, rural and indigenous social movements.

In the year 2000 in Brazil we won major electoral victories in almost 200 municipalities, including seven state capitals. Our victories were based on a popular and democratic front of political parties, which also sought to represent environmental, feminist and urban social movements. For us it was proof that this is the fundamental, strategic social base underpinning a programme for social change, for a real break with underdevelopment and a transition to socialism.

If this is possible in municipalities, large and small, it is also possible in our countries' states and provinces, based on a programmatic identification with the interests of the majority of the population.

Such results are particularly important given the history of the left in Brazil and in Latin America, with its long subordination to populism and cross-class alliances. They help consolidate the policy of alliances needed to put an anti-neoliberal, anti-capitalist programme into practice.

Nothing could be more urgent for a continent in deep crisis as a consequence of structural dependence and the devastation wrought by the foreign debt. We are already seeing ruling-class governments overthrown by desperate, spontaneous action of the popular masses, thanks to their own historic inability to defend national sovereignty at all.

May our local experiences and the World Social Forum help the peoples of Latin America and other continents practically and theoretically, so that they become the protagonists of this new world.

9

The Question of Democracy Today[1]

Raul Pont

The theme of this seminar panel, 'The Lula Government and Socialism', obliges us to concentrate on just a few issues. A variety of other topics may of course come up in the discussion. That's fine by me. But I want to prioritise the discussion around an issue that seems to me to offer us the best chance of exerting influence where we are active.

If our central, almost obsessive, aim is to defend, consolidate and improve the balance of forces so that we can advance further, then I believe that our over-riding concern at present should be extending democracy in Brazil. Some may think that now that we have the president and a sizeable group in parliament,[2] the democratic struggle is just a matter of ensuring respect for the rules of the game. But I want to address the issue from a broader, programmatic and strategic point of view. Tackling the question of democracy does not mean limiting ourselves to reproducing the representative system. We know very well that the classic liberal state we have inherited from previous centuries was and remains the political expression of capitalist domination.

The struggle to extend democracy is important for the left everywhere, not just in underdeveloped countries. In general the left around the world is weak, theoretically and programmatically, on this question. Socialist thought has not come very far in its critique of the representative system. Experiences of democracy in the countries of 'really existing socialism' were ephemeral or non-existent.

Without wishing any offence to our European visitors, there are countries in Europe, which we call the First World, where we still see monarchies, where some people are born noble, born unequal – something that republican liberals tried to put an end to in the eighteenth century.

This shows that the struggle for democracy is a live issue in all bourgeois societies. In the Brazilian case, this is aggravated by the legacy of colonial slavery, underdevelopment and a bourgeoisie that has always been submissive, first in the colonial epoch to Portugal, later to Britain and more recently to the US and the centres of international capital. The left has produced very little in this area. Its vision and understanding of democratic issues have often been limited.

In the second half of the nineteenth century, the achievement of trade-union and party organisation and the right to political representation brought a series of social and political victories and reforms that contributed to seeing the representative system as an important tool for winning social demands. The project coming out of the 1917 Russian Revolution for governments based on 'councils' (soviets) did not spread to the rest of Europe and lasted only briefly in a Russia that had hardly any experience of the liberal representative system.

Throughout the twentieth century and especially during the Stalinist period in the Soviet Union, the dominant attitude towards democracy among socialists was a utilitarian one. Very little attention was given to how masses of people could really become the subjects of society, to the control of public affairs by the great majority. The unbreakable link between democracy and socialism was forgotten. Nobody did the theoretical or programmatic work that would point towards replacing bourgeois democracy with experiences based on self-management, recallable mandates, a reduction in the delegation of power and more direct forms of control over public spending and the state. What predominated was a simplistic vision of 'bourgeois dictatorship' versus 'dictatorship of the proletariat'.

In Brazil, the left's backward approach to democracy was revealed in the debate about an amnesty for political prisoners during the military dictatorship. The older ones among you may remember that shortly before the PT was founded, when we still had political prisoners in Brazil, we went through a debate in which some people insisted – and this is in the documents written at the time – that struggling for an amnesty and in defence of political prisoners was wrong and a waste of time. For them the political prisoner was a fighter in enemy hands. When 'our turn came' we would pay them back in kind. Quite simply, the dictatorship of the proletariat would supersede the dictatorship of the bourgeoisie.

This made it difficult to carry out concrete struggles and develop greater popular participation. It trapped many of us in a purely doctrinaire position. Even after the PT emerged, this debate continued. We spent two or three years in the PT discussing whether the constituent assembly was or wasn't an adequate slogan to sum up the popular movement's alternative to the military dictatorship. Thousands and thousands of words of documents and theses were written to prove that this would be a simple surrender to bourgeois ideology, that the masses had no interest in such questions because 'you can't eat a constituent assembly'.

So as we see, we suffer from a huge programmatic weakness on the question of democracy. Nonetheless, if we really want to think about changing the balance of forces and broadening the very restricted space that we operate in, then we need more than anything to have popular participation and support. People's concrete social struggles and the victories they win by mobilising around things like housing, wages and unemployment, as well as their experience in our local governments of deciding how the city's money should be spent, are fundamental to guaranteeing a change in the balance of forces.

Popular participation is essential if people are to develop a clearer understanding, in each struggle and at every stage, of how municipal governments, state governments and the national state itself all work – of who decides on taxes, how tax revenues are split up, who pays and who doesn't.

This demands a huge effort from us. We must build mechanisms that can make the link in practice between the struggle for socialism and the extension of democracy. This is precisely where our struggle for the participatory budget comes in, along with strengthening and giving real decisionmaking power to the municipal and state councils[3] and other, more direct forms of popular participation.

But unfortunately, many of our PT local governments simply reproduce classic representative democracy, limited to the delegation of power to city councillors and mayors. This approach to politics suffers from all the familiar problems of bureaucracy and fraud generated by parties, candidates and the electoral system itself.

In opposition to this, and taking account of the real circumstances and possibilities that face us, we need to insist that another kind of democracy is possible. That means thinking through at every stage what other kind of democracy we can implant and develop, in accordance with people's lived experience and level of awareness.

In the debate over the Lula government and how it will win support, I see no sign of any policies to extend democracy and popular participation as key elements in winning such support. On the contrary, all the government team's early efforts seem directed towards building a coalition of centre and even conservative parties in order to achieve a majority in Congress. All the reports in the press of negotiations with fractions and dissident currents of this or that party indicate that this is the path that has been chosen – to give the government room to manoeuvre and get its legislation through.

In my view this tactic will run into problems. It will tie us to conservative parties and politicians who are long-schooled in corruption and influence peddling. They will make us pay dearly, politically and financially, for their votes. They will seek to protect the social and regional interests they represent.

There is another way. Encouraging and strengthening people's participation in discussing and deciding the direction of public policies is a real and possible alternative. Brazil's presidential system gives the executive considerable scope for initiative in the areas of taxation and the budget. This is something we have learned through our city administrations and here in the state of Rio Grande do Sul.

This does not imply abandoning Congress or ruling out tactical agreements to approve specific projects. It is not about sidelining our representatives and senators, much less about wanting 'to close Congress down'. But there are serious problems with limiting the question of government and government support to winning victories in a Congress that has an in-built conservative majority.

As well as signalling a desire for good relations and peaceful co-existence with parliament, we should be sending out very clear signals to the Landless Workers' Movement, the CUT and other trade union federations, to all the social, community, student and anti-discrimination movements.

We should propose to the movements that they meet, mobilise and decide on public policies that we will implement. We should not be frightened of talking directly to the movements or of creating forums and other mechanisms for direct, popular participation. This is where real support for the government will come from.

This is not a route that implies 'building barricades against Bush' right now, or an immediate break with the IMF and World Bank. Nor can it be claimed that it requires resources we don't have. What it does require is the political will. It requires a programmatic vision that this is a process of transition that really can overcome underdevelopment.

The experience in Porto Alegre and the popular democratic government in Rio Grande do Sul show that this process allows thousands of citizens to mobilise in defence of the material interests they share as exploited members of society. They want quality public services in healthcare, education and social services. They're ready to struggle for this, and they understand that their government, which they elected, will put the resources at their disposal.

Everyone here knows that we didn't lose the 2002 elections for state governor because of the participatory budget and the participatory democracy we were practising. In fact it was this that allowed us, in spite of the mistakes we made in the electoral campaign, to obtain the same number of votes as in 1998, when we won by a tiny margin in a highly polarised state, where our political enemies are strong. And of course this is a vitally important lesson in politics – to recognise who really are your enemies, and how strong they are.

The experience of participatory democracy in Rio Grande and Porto Alegre made it possible for us to build on our traditional layers of support – urban and rural workers and youth – and extend the legitimacy and hegemony of our political project among other sections of society. Our relationship with small business people changed, for example. A number of such sectors drew closer, developed trust and came to believe in what we were doing.

The reason for our victories in Porto Alegre over the last 15 years has been precisely the fact that we have handed power back to the people that the representative system delegates to the mayor and municipal departmental heads. We have returned to them, organised in assemblies, the power to decide what to do with the public purse.

In my opinion it is through this democratic struggle, through opening up spaces for participatory democracy and inviting the people themselves to take the lead, that change can be achieved more quickly and more deeply. That is why the Lula government, *our* government, should encourage popular participation and make it the government's top political priority, as a means of building a new political hegemony in Brazil.

Finally, I'd like to refer to the question of political reform. I think we need to make a huge effort to ensure that it is the issue of democracy that shapes our approach to this debate. We need to take the initiative in this discussion of political reform. We need to reject all forms of 'first-past-the-post' voting systems, as well as the electoral swindle carried out in Brazil under the guise of a completely distorted proportional representation in parliament. In our country this produces first-, second- and third-class citizens. We haven't even come as far as the French Revolution and 'one person, one vote'. States in Brazil still function as electoral colleges, with their minimum and maximum numbers of representatives carried over from the military regime. As a result the representation of citizens in parliament is a fraud.

We need to connect the debate on political reform with an understanding of the importance of extending democracy for our ability to lead a major political transformation in this country. This means building into our programme the quest for new political institutions and a whole new conception of the executive and legislature and their relations with society.

The question of democracy should be the guiding principle of all our political activity. For example, the struggle to decentralise administration is linked to our understanding of socialism. We do not seek a society governed from an all-powerful Brasilia, with all-powerful federal ministries. Our struggle is also a struggle for decentralisation, and for ever more direct control by citizens in the municipalities over public resources.

This commitment to the struggle for democracy, to a new logic of democracy, should shape everything we do, our relations with our supporters and with social movements, and the policies of our popular local governments. It is the starting point for a transition that will demand equally daring proposals and policies to deal with the economy and the world of work.

10
PT Local Governments and Socialism

João Machado[1]

During the last century, the balance sheet of governments calling themselves socialist was a big disappointment. This goes for both those identifying with the Russian Revolution and its various offshoots and those usually called social democratic. The outcomes of the former, following the collapse of the Soviet Union and its former satellites, are catastrophic (however much we may value the efforts of those like Cuba to keep going). The results of social democratic governments, though more nuanced – after all in a number of countries they did carry out reforms that improved people's living conditions, and these achievements have not completely disappeared – should also be seen as negative. In recent decades social democratic governments have become social-liberal governments. There has been a rollback of the rights won after the Second World War, and it has become difficult to make any clear distinction between social democracy and the prevailing neoliberalism.

This disappointing balance sheet does not mean that the chapter of socialist experiences is closed, however. In a way this current period, dominated by governments fully identified with capitalism, its values and methods, has shown just how little this kind of society has to offer humanity.

For most of the 1990s, the idea was promoted that the world was entering a new phase of solid technical progress, free from the old recurrent crises: the so-called 'new economy'. It is clear now that this claim was baseless. Instead the discussion is again going back and forth between how long the current downturn will last and how strong the next upturn will prove. True, the 1980s and 1990s were exceptionally favourable for the capitalist economy. Yet even its best years did not lead to an improvement in living standards for the majority of people on the planet. Even then capitalism offered most people very little.

Even before the latest recession there was worldwide pressure to cut back on social rights and make jobs less secure. At the same time demands on the workforce were increasing, for higher qualifications, more intensive labour processes and longer working days. Even then many jobs paid less than they had before. Even then, in the name of competitiveness, more was being asked of workers, while less was being paid for their labour. Everyone was being asked to run faster and faster, in the hope of, just maybe, staying in the same place. And what made the situation worse for the majority of the world's population in this epoch of globalised capitalism was that the gap between rich countries and poor countries was growing broader and deeper. Now, with the system's tendency towards recession taking over once again, these negative features of the capitalist economy have only grown sharper.

The deceptive nature of capitalism's promises shows that the search for alternatives has lost none of its relevance. However the double disappointment in the Soviet model and social democracy has made it very difficult to defend a socialist alternative. For Third World countries there is an additional factor to consider. In the years when neoliberal capitalism held greatest sway, there was a growing belief that one possibly progressive variant within capitalism – 'national developmentalism' – had also turned out to be a failure since the 1980s. Many people in Brazil asserted that the second national development plan, the last big attempt to promote a relatively independent, 'national' kind of Brazilian capitalist development, had been partly responsible for the debt crisis and the 'lost decade' of the 1980s.

The upshot is that, however little promise capitalism holds out today, it has been very difficult to argue for anything different, or even to propose changes within the dominant model.

In this context the different experiences of local government by the Brazilian Workers' Party (PT), especially in Porto Alegre and Rio Grande do Sul, take on very great importance.

When the PT won the mayoral election in Porto Alegre in 1988, it was a party with very particular characteristics. It identified wholeheartedly with the socialist cause, yet was critical of both the Soviet Union and the experiences of social democratic governments. At the same time it was convinced that the road to power would go through elections, depending on victories like its victories that year in a number of cities (and later in states). It believed that success would depend on demonstrating its administrative ability, whilst also showing that it could govern differently from Brazil's traditional parties or social democratic parties in other countries.

But the PT's commitment to a democratic road did not mean that its strategy was limited to standing in elections. Popular organisation and strengthening the social movements were also central to the PT's vision. Nor did the party idealise liberal democratic institutions. There was a broadly shared conviction in the party of the need to go beyond their limitations.

Furthermore the PT in Rio Grande do Sul had particularities of its own, linked to the state's traditionally high level of political awareness. On the one hand, party life was more active and organised than in most of the country. On the other, left currents were stronger here inside the PT than in most other states.

After 1989, the year the PT administration took office in Porto Alegre, the PT suffered from the international crisis of the left following the collapse of the so-called 'socialist camp'. This was felt in Rio Grande do Sul as well. But the relatively high level of political awareness in Rio Grande do Sul and the strength of the PT left wing, though undermined, remained.

Thus at the beginning of 1989 the PT in Porto Alegre had a clearer understanding of the challenge ahead than it did in other cities it was beginning to govern. It knew it had to find new ways of running things.[2] And when the proposal to hold a World Social Forum was first put forward in 2000, the PT in Rio Grande do Sul was more open to understanding its importance and giving it a decisive push forward.[3]

Other chapters in this book have analysed the innovations developed in Porto Alegre, and later in other cities and the state of Rio Grande do Sul, especially the participatory budget. My aim here is different: to consider how the experience of different PT local governments, especially in Porto Alegre and Rio Grande do Sul, can be connected to the attempt in recent years to renew the socialist project. The extent to which it can contribute to this vital task is probably one of the most important aspects of this rich experience.

This does not mean however that all those active in PT local governments across Brazil, or even in Rio Grande do Sul, share the ideas presented here. Even in Rio Grande, although those responsible for local administrations there share the concern with linking what the PT has achieved to proposals for renewing socialist thought, their views vary considerably. This chapter makes suggestions that go beyond what has been put into practice or even proposed by the

PT so far in Rio Grande do Sul. Some of the questions raised below clearly could only be applied at the national level. They are therefore part of the debate the PT as a whole faces in its discussions of the Lula government.[4]

Nonetheless, there is a clear link between these ideas and the experiences of the various PT administrations. The link can be summed up in the following question: *what would a socialist strategy look like in which these innovations in local government played a central role?*

To put it another way: the starting point of the ideas expressed here is the conviction that a socialist party in government must never restrict itself to administering capitalism. This is true even when the balance of forces does not allow a break with bourgeois rule, even when the government in question is only a municipal administration, suffering all the limitations inherent in local government. Even at this level a socialist party's socialist objectives must inform its programme. Its programme must link up somehow with its socialist goal.

THE NEOLIBERAL ARGUMENT

After the collapse of the USSR and its 'socialist camp', it is clearly necessary to rethink the socialist project in the light of that experience. It is equally important – though less often remembered – to rethink the project in the light of the failures of social democracy. Social democracy may have contributed to important advances in a number of countries for several decades. But for the last 20 years or more it has not represented any real alternative. It has turned into 'social-liberalism', a variant of neoliberalism. In reality, even in its heyday social democracy never lived up to its most ambitious aims (or the aims of its most ambitious supporters); it was never a road for the transition to socialism.[5] It also never proved to be a viable current in the Third World. For our present purposes, the limitations of social democracy are even more important than those of the Soviet model.

Before exploring how we can renew the socialist project, we can examine briefly the criticisms that its opponents, especially neoliberals, have levelled at it. The kernel of recent neoliberal ideology is contained in the binary opposition: *inefficient and anti-democratic statism versus the efficient and democratic market* – as if these were the only two options available to society. From this point of view, any form of socialism (or developmentalism, or indeed anything besides neoliberalism) is seen as 'statist', and subject to all the attendant ills.

The fact that 'statism' has indeed been a central feature of most versions of socialism to date – the 'really existing socialism' of the USSR as well as social democracy – has contributed to the remarkable spread of this dogma. Despite their differences, both these major currents in the workers' movement had a bureaucratic character, aiming to use the state to change society from the top down. In the first case, a new state apparatus was built, ultra-centralised, authoritarian and identified with the party in power. Any independent initiative by the people was seen as dangerous and subversive.

Social democratic currents, on the other hand, adapted to the existing, capitalist state apparatus. They made minor changes to it and aimed to use it in favour of the majority of the people, while avoiding any direct confrontation with capital. This meant rejecting any autonomous participation by the people, restricting popular participation to what is possible within the framework of bourgeois democratic institutions. Anything going beyond these limits has been repressed. Admittedly there has been much less direct state repression under social democratic governments than under Soviet-style regimes.[6] But social democracy has combined a relatively lower level of repression with the restrictions on freedom and democracy that flow from the operation of the market itself (a subject we will return to).

The two versions of 'social statism' were thus both undemocratic. This was obvious in the Soviet model, though not for the reasons identified by the neoliberal critique. (For example, neoliberals argue that not recognising companies' property rights is fundamentally undemocratic.) As for the social democratic model, its undemocratic characteristics are largely the opposite of those indicated by the neoliberal critique. It has not been able to go *beyond* the liberal representative system. It shares the achievements and the limitations of this form of democracy, in particular the subordination of social choices to the rule of the market.

The argument about inefficiency is more questionable. True, both the Soviet and social democratic models were utterly inefficient ways of building socialist societies. But if we judge them by neoliberal critics' own criteria, in terms of their ability to promote economic growth, then their inefficiency is much more relative. For several decades, economic growth in the USSR was high. The same was true of social democracy. For our purposes, however, the main point is that both forms of 'social statism' involve fundamental limitations on democracy and are therefore of no use as alternative projects.[7]

On the other hand, the experience of the last few decades shows that the other side of the neoliberal formula, the 'democratic and efficient market', does not stand up. World economic growth in the 1980s and 1990s, the decades in which neoliberalism held sway, was less than half that in the 'statist' 1950s and 1960s. The 'social inefficiency' of neoliberalism is even greater than its economic inefficiency: unemployment is twice or three times as high as in the 1950s and 1960s; income distribution has become more unequal; real wages have tended to stagnate or fall; there have been cuts in pensions, social security and social rights in general. None of this is accidental. The drive to be 'competitive' leads to a race to reduce labour costs, which produces permanent pressure to reduce workers' rights, make employment more precarious and cut pensions and social security.

The supposed ability of private companies to deliver public services more efficiently is not being borne out. And however hard dependent countries work to 'merit' the confidence of international markets, they have not only failed to enjoy the 'fruits' of globalisation, they have ended up more vulnerable to crises, more dependent and less in control of their own affairs. The situation of Brazil leaves no room for doubt about this. In terms of efficiency, then, the balance sheet is clear: neoliberal capitalism is incapable of offering people what 'statist' capitalism gave them for several decades.

In terms of democracy, neoliberalism's performance is even worse. Far from favouring democracy, *the growing dominance of deregulated markets leads to a greater and greater reduction in democratic rights*. One of the guiding principles of neoliberal governments' theory and practice is the need to 'win the confidence' of markets in general and financial markets in particular. That is, neoliberal governments guarantee that nothing will be done against the markets' interests. Any whiff of a change in economic policies, any suggestion that measures might be implemented that are not in the interests of the 'financial community', provokes 'pressure from investors'. Apart from being wholly undemocratic, this rides roughshod over national sovereignty – without which, of course, there can be no progress towards democracy anyway.

The bill to be paid for 'winning confidence' is a hefty one. Public spending on social needs (education, health, sanitation, housing and infrastructure) is cut in order to increase governments' ability to pay usurious interest rates to domestic and foreign creditors. As if 'investors' pressure' were not enough, economic policymakers are required to accept supervision by the IMF, an ever more direct representative of the interests of the great powers, especially the United States, and of finance capital.

Perhaps the most clearly undemocratic aspect of the neoliberal logic is its treatment of employment. Since neoliberal policies keep global demand stagnant, technical progress – which should allow everyone to work less, produce more, and therefore enjoy more leisure and higher consumption – ends up making some people work more without earning any more, whilst others lose their jobs. What is democratic about a worker with ten or twenty years in a company being laid off, without any discussion or vote, so that the company can maintain its profits and its 'competitive edge'?

The dictatorship of the markets is the chief enemy of democracy today. The characteristic neoliberal claim that the need to respond to the markets drastically reduces the room for political decisions represents a frontal attack on citizens' sovereign right to decide their own destiny.

Yet neoliberals do not, in reality, advocate weaker states. They want in theory to reduce states' economic role, without eliminating it – states should still guarantee the operation of the market, respect for property rights and contracts, etc., all of which are key economic functions. In reality the state remains an important source of subsidies and cheap credit for big capital, as seen in Ford's decision to leave Rio Grande do Sul when the new PT government refused to honour the exceedingly generous subsidies and tax breaks offered by its predecessor. The state is also assigned the role of handing over large chunks of public property to private interests, foreign and domestic, through privatisation.[8]

Even more obviously, neoliberals need states to be well armed in order to 'guarantee order'. It is no accident that the Pinochet dictatorship in Chile and the Videla dictatorship in Argentina were pioneers of the neoliberal wave.

RENEWING THE SOCIALIST PROJECT

Perhaps the best way of organising discussion about a new project is to go back to the basic ideas that inspired the early socialists, especially Marx. They offer a good way of combining opposition to the now dominant ideology with a critique of the actual historical experiences that have called themselves socialist. They suggest that socialism must be built in opposition to both the state and the capitalist market. That is, socialism requires opposing regulation of the economy by the market, and in particular the exploitation of labour that occurs when capital and wage labour confront each other in the labour market.

This approach views the state as a power that restricts the self-organisation of society in a way that benefits the economically and politically dominant class, and the market not as a source of freedom but as an impersonal power that subordinates individuals to a logic beyond their control in order to constantly increase the value of capital. Both state and market restrict the liberty of all citizens. This restriction is asymmetrical, however: it hits workers and other popular sectors the hardest.

We therefore need to reject the choice on offer between state and market. We need to reject statism, because it is an attempt to bring about social change from the top down, with popular participation controlled by the state apparatus. And we need to reject the rule of the market, because it subordinates popular needs to an alien logic that favours capital. Socialism can only be based on human solidarity as a fundamental value and the ability of citizens to decide their own destiny – in other words, on self-government by workers and other citizens.

If we want to defend socialism as an alternative today, we need to understand it as the organised population increasing its control over the mechanisms of economic and political management in society, and creating the conditions for solidarity to replace competition as the basic form of relations between human beings. This means creating institutions based on the 'free association of producers' and people's autonomous, democratic and sovereign activity, which must occupy spaces currently taken up by the capitalist market and state.

For the long term, we can retain Marx's idea that a truly free society will have eliminated commodity production, along with the market and all mercantile categories and the state as a separate political apparatus. For the time being however our aim is a more limited one, even though it *does lead in this direction*. It is to develop all possible forms of popular self-organisation and social control over both state and market.

In this approach, *everything that strengthens the awareness and self-organisation of workers and people in general*; everything that escapes the dichotomy between vertical control by the state on the one hand and passive citizenship on the other; everything that contradicts the logic of competition and the market and instead favours cooperation and planning of shared interests and fosters values of equality, genuine democracy and solidarity *sets us on the path towards socialism*. The core of this process can be summed up in one simple idea – *full democratisation of society* – meaning citizens coming together to control everything that affects their common destiny.

Although we need to be clear about our opposition to both the capitalist market and state, the criticism cannot be made symmetrically. In the here and now it is possible to propose neither the disappearance of the state – that is obvious – nor its reduction. What we do need is to transform it, so that it is increasingly controlled by an organised and conscious population, and therefore increasingly becomes a genuine *res publica*, a 'thing of the people'. In this sense we do need to weaken the state – its domination over the body of society.

THE PT EXPERIENCE: THE LOCAL LEVEL

From this point of view it is possible to advance towards socialism even on the basis of local and state governments. This is one of the most important lessons of the experience in Porto Alegre and other PT administrations, even in a situation where the overall balance of forces did not favour the building of socialism. The concrete experience of developing forms of popular participation – especially the participatory budget – in various municipalities, spreading later to the state of Rio Grande do Sul, backs up this view.

In the first place, this experience has shown that establishing social control over the state is not only democratic but also efficient. As socialist theoretician Ernest Mandel liked to point out, changes in the field of communications and information technology have dramatically reduced the difficulties of practising participatory democracy. They make it much easier to take the discussion of key questions for every level of society (national, regional and local) to all citizens, making decisionmaking ever more direct.

Second, there is a very clear connection between this way of managing public resources and a renewed conception of socialism. It develops popular self-organisation and challenges citizens' passivity. It broadens people's awareness of the limitations of the state, of contradictions between classes and so on. All this goes towards reducing the state's domination over citizens.

Third, this experience helps train technical cadres in a popular and democratic conception of public administration – something that is absolutely vital for any eventual transition to socialism involving the reabsorption of the state by society.

Another way that PT local governments have pointed towards creating conditions for a socialist alternative has been the support given to all kinds of economic self-organisation and self-management. This includes different kinds of cooperatives and other forms of collective endeavour often referred to as an 'economy of cooperation and solidarity'.

The cooperative movement has been growing in Brazil in recent years. This has come from two directions. In the countryside, the Landless Workers' Movement (MST) has encouraged those who obtain land to organise themselves in cooperatives; they see cooperatives as part of their longstanding commitment to link the struggle for land to the struggle for socialism. In the cities, unemployment has been prompting workers to seek alternatives to the companies they used to work for – including by forming cooperatives. One of the most interesting forms of urban cooperative is when workers take over companies that have gone bust and been abandoned by their owners. There is a countrywide organisation now giving technical assistance to such cooperatives, the Association of Workers in Self-Managed Enterprises.

Strengthening an 'economy of cooperation and solidarity' contributes in a number of ways to developing a socialist alternative. It raises the level of workers' organisation, develops their experience of management and makes them more capable of governing themselves, showing at the same time that bosses are not indispensable. It strengthens a cooperative, and therefore socialist, vision of the world. It also broadens the part of the economy outside the logic of capitalism; that is, it weakens the capitalist market logic and strengthens a logic of solidarity that points towards socialism.

Of course, within a capitalist economy cooperatives come under pressure to adapt to the market. Often they do not keep their anti-capitalist character.[9] Even genuine cooperatives can be pushed towards adopting a business mentality, and imitating the relationship between capital and labour. The big challenge is to demonstrate that efficiency is not to be confused with market competitiveness. State support, or other kinds of public backing, for cooperatives (through granting favourable terms of credit and providing technical assistance and help with distribution) is one way of reducing the pressure of the market. Indeed this kind of support was an important policy of the PT government in Rio Grande do Sul, and has featured in other PT administrations as well. The CUT trade union federation has adopted the same policy.

THE NATIONAL LEVEL

The socialist strategy outlined above cannot be fully implemented at the level of municipal and state governments, even though it can begin there. The state must be democratised and participatory democracy developed at the national level too – even if it is not immediately possible to break with the domination of the bourgeoisie. The same goes, of course, for encouraging the development of an 'economy of solidarity'.[10]

One key socialist policy that takes place essentially at the national level is state coordination of economic activity. In direct opposition to the neoliberal mantra, we have to reject the idea that the economy should be regulated mainly by the market. In *macroeconomic policy*, a socialist approach can critically reappropriate the Keynesian and developmentalist agendas that prevailed from the end of the Second World War to the 1970s. Keynes argued that the state needs to correct the workings of the markets, particularly so as to make up for the market's 'failure to provide for full employment and its arbitrary and inequitable distribution of wealth and incomes'.[11] He recommended regular government intervention to sustain aggregate demand and therefore the level of employment, keep interest rates low, create jobs and reduce excessive disparities in the distribution of income and wealth.

In this way official economic policy was *politicised*. It became a matter of interest to everyone. Trade unions discussed it, not just bankers. It became clear that macroeconomic policy is not neutral, but can favour the interests of one class or another. In this respect the neoliberal wave that swept the world in the 1980s was a great leap backwards.

Besides macroeconomic policy, the national state needs to coordinate economic activity through a series of sectoral policies to ensure that economic activity matches social needs (which the market never spontaneously meets). While we may not be able to eliminate the market in the foreseeable future, we can control it socially. For the time being that must mean control by state bodies *under popular control*. From a democratic point of view, just as cutting back the state in order to give free reign to the markets takes away much of people's power to decide, there is no point in strengthening the state unless we extend the mechanisms by which society can control the state. On the other hand, strengthened state intervention accompanied by social control over state activity increases citizens' power to decide their own living conditions, and therefore increases democracy. In the long run it can even point towards the disappearance of the state – that is, to its reabsorption by organised society.

Such state coordination of economic activity should ensure an ever-greater reduction in social and regional inequalities and encourage socialising technical progress.[12] This does not require nationalising the whole economy, but it does require a significant public sector. Given the privatisations pushed through in recent years, this means combining renationalisation of a number of companies with forms of social control. Especially in the big companies, relations must be changed inside capitalist firms themselves, *extending workers' rights in the face of capital*. One of the first measures should be to limit companies' unrestricted right to lay off workers.

Other key questions at national level are pensions, healthcare and social services, together one of the biggest challenges of the present period. All countries have come under heavy neoliberal pressure to cut back the space expressing values of solidarity and expand the space given over to the market by privatising services and pensions. On the contrary, strengthening the public character of social services and the spirit of solidarity should be a key axis of socialist strategy.

All these economic changes would imply a change in the class balance of forces, in workers' favour and to capital's detriment. They would open the economy to a process of conflict between the still-dominant logic of the market and the logic of social needs – a conflict that could put the economy's capitalist character in question.

THE INTERNATIONAL LEVEL

Socialist strategy also includes an international dimension, of course. In recent decades, neoliberal globalisation has deepened dependent countries' submission to the imperial centres. A real process of recolonisation is under way. In this respect the historical retreat has been particularly brutal. Efforts made over several decades under pressure from popular movements, to give a more 'national' character to economic and political decisionmaking in the countries of the periphery, are being swept away.

The first international aspect of a socialist project in the Third World is thus the struggle for national sovereignty. This has several aspects: rejecting IMF and World Bank tutelage, fighting against foreign debt (for example by suspending payments and doing an audit of the terms on which the debt was contracted), controlling capital flows, reviewing privatisations (most of which have benefited foreign capital), and limiting repatriation of profits by multinationals.

Defending sovereignty needs to be combined with the struggle for a different international order. There is absolutely no possibility of dependent countries' participating in the current world order whilst preserving their sovereignty. To the globalisation of capital and markets we must oppose the solidarity and internationalism of peoples. International relations must not be surrendered to the logic of deregulated markets. They must be consciously built by each country, through bilateral agreements and appropriate forums for negotiation.

This is precisely what the international movement against neoliberal globalisation that has emerged over the last few years calls 'another globalisation' or 'deglobalisation'. It is not by chance that this movement has found one of its strongest sources of support in Porto Alegre and the World Social Forums first held there. On the one hand, PT activists from Rio Grande do Sul and other parts of Brazil found in the movement a natural partner in their quest for a renewal of socialist strategy. On the other, activists from other countries saw initiatives like the participatory budget as a demonstration that it is possible to begin moving towards another kind of society.

PERMANENT TENSION

Any strategy that tries to advance towards socialism while starting from local, regional or even national governments, in conditions where an immediate revolutionary break with the existing institutions is not yet possible, runs a risk of adaptation and distortion. For this reason, even in the most favourable scenario of a simultaneous advance on all the levels mentioned above, there is *an inevitable tension between the achievements realised and the still dominant logic of the capitalist market*. In fact, *the existence of this tension can serve as a barometer of whether the socialist impulse is still present or not*.

This tension touches basic economic and social structures as well as the workings of state power. It cannot be a result of governmental action alone. There must be simultaneous pressure from within and from without. Just as important as winning elections therefore is forming what has become known in the PT tradition as the 'democratic and popular bloc'. Nor is it enough to develop this bloc as an electoral force, to win elections and occupy positions in the institutions. It also needs to achieve growing levels of organisation and mobilisation in society at large, in an ideological and cultural battle over the basic direction society is heading in.[13] Values of solidarity within the national community and the community of nations need to become dominant values. This fight over values will be decisive in counteracting the pressure to adapt to the capitalist economic order and existing state institutions. In other words, we need a socialist movement that can serve as an ideological and ethical framework and a source of social and economic support for all the different kinds of struggle.

At a time when neoliberal ideas seem to rule the world, with their cult of the individual, competition and 'looking out for number one', it may seem futile to try and base any proposal on the idea of increased solidarity. Nonetheless, we have an important example that shows these ideas can work: the success of the Landless Workers' Movement (MST). The MST is built on solidarity, and it has proved that this is a solid foundation. It has won widespread sympathy both in Brazil and internationally. Part or all of that sympathy is precisely a result of the values that it defends and practises.

Curiously enough, the idea of advancing towards socialism while starting from local, regional or even national governments, in conditions where a revolutionary break with existing institutions is not yet possible, has been criticised in the PT from both the right and the left. The criticisms 'from the left' have taken various forms. Some have focused on experiences like the participatory budget or overlapped with criticisms of the World Social Forums. Their basic argument seems to be a somewhat schematic insistence on the need for revolution and rejection of any kind of gradualism in the transformation of society. According to this view, prior to the establishment of a socialist state the task is simply to mobilise workers around their various demands.

In response to these criticisms it is important to emphasise that the vision laid out here is not opposed to the need for a revolutionary break with the present order. On the contrary, the accumulation of popular organisation and administrative experience through processes like the participatory budget greatly increases the possibility of such a break.[14] More important still, it greatly increases the chances of avoiding the kinds of deformation that have characterised many revolutionary experiences ever since the Russian Revolution.

Clearly socialist parties like the PT *can* win municipal, regional and even national elections and assume governmental responsibilities at these different levels, even when the balance of forces rules out an immediate revolutionary break. In this situation, we basically have three options. First, we can adopt an apparently radical stance that quickly makes it impossible to remain in government. Second, we can adopt a programme that accepts the restrictions of the capitalist framework. Or third, we can work with the situation as it exists, but seek to build bridges towards a socialist transformation.[15]

The third alternative makes the most sense. If a socialist party is able to win office even on the unfavourable playing field of bourgeois elections, then some space must have opened up for change. In this case the best thing to do is to try to make changes that move forward in the direction of socialism – not just out of ideological preference, but because socialist policies are more effective and serve people's interests better.

This may not be possible if we think of it only in terms of a revolutionary break; but it may be perfectly possible if we define socialism as we did above, as the *full democratisation of society*. To repeat what we have already said: *everything that strengthens the awareness and self-organisation of workers and people in general;* everything that escapes the dichotomy between vertical control by the state on the one hand and passive citizenship on the other hand; everything that contradicts the logic of competition and the market and instead favours cooperation and planning of shared interests and fosters values of equality, genuine democracy and solidarity *sets us on the path towards socialism.*

Notes

INTRODUCTION

1. 'Another world is possible' – the central slogan of the World Social Forums
   held in Porto Alegre in 2001, 2002 and 2003 before moving to Mumbai
   in India in 2004 – became a chorus of the global justice movement in
   its many different forms.

PROLOGUE

1. The following community leaders and activists from the Gloria region
   of Porto Alegre took part in this discussion:

   Edimar Silveira – Graciliano Neighbourhood Association
   Nilven Trinidade – Parque Tabajara Neighbourhood Association
   José Brizola – Participatory Budget Councillor
   Sirley Vargas – Nossa Senhora de Lourdes Neighbourhood
   Association
   Heloisa Vinola – Belem Velho Community Association
   Silvio Arce – Coordination of Popular Movements

1 PARTICIPATORY DEMOCRACY – THE DEBATE

1. Raul Pont was one of the PT's founders and has become one of the best-
   known architects and exponents of the participatory budget. In 2001
   he was the main left candidate for the post of party president, coming
   second with 17.5 per cent of the vote to 55 per cent for José Dirceu, who
   later became President Lula's chief of staff. Pont is also a leader of the
   Socialist Democracy (DS) tendency within the PT.
2. The military dictatorship in Brazil, from 1964 to 1984, had been more
   sophisticated than most of its kin in other parts of Latin America. It
   maintained a functioning, though powerless, national congress, with
   periodic elections and two official parties. It also maintained elected
   local governments, though not in the state capitals, where the mayors
   were nominated.
3. The strength of the radical church in this part of Brazil was also a factor
   in the parallel growth of the Landless Workers' Movement (MST), which
   emerged in Rio Grande do Sul in the mid 1980s out of the work of the
   Catholic Church's Pastoral Land Commission.
4. Different strands of the organised left had also played a part in Diadema
   and in Fortaleza, but their influence was less deeply rooted and less
   longlasting than in Porto Alegre.
5. Originating from the Sino-Soviet split in the 1960s, the PCdoB eventually
   discarded its ideological references to Mao Zedong as well as its later

identification with Albanian leader Enver Hoxha. It remained the largest left party outside the PT, with which it has maintained an electoral alliance since the early 1980s. Its consistent grassroots activism in the social movements and its small but significant parliamentary presence have combined with a strategic perspective that was often to the right of the PT's, giving great weight to an alliance with the 'national bourgeoisie'.

6. The group which José Dirceu had been close to, though not a member of, was Action for National Liberation, led by the legendary Carlos Marighela, a former leader of the Moscow-line Communist Party. Killed in a shootout with the police in 1969, Marighela had written a manual on urban guerrilla warfare that became an important reference for armed groups in other countries, including the Weather Underground and others in the US.

7. Antonio Palocci, like President Lula's communications director Luis Gushiken, is a former leader of the Freedom and Struggle (*Liberdade e Luta*) current, linked to the Trotskyist current of Pierre Lambert in France, which played a significant part in the early days of the PT but later lost most of its influence.

8. Socialist Democracy was created at the end of the 1970s by the merger of several small groups of militants either attracted to or already identifying with the Fourth International. The most significant were a group of students in Minas Gerais state and the group in Porto Alegre around Raul Pont.

9. See Carlos Rossi, 'Assessing the Nicaraguan Elections', and Ernest Mandel, 'Road to "Socialist Democracy"', both in *Intercontinental Press* vol. 22, no. 24 (24 December 1984); and Charles-André Udry, 'The Sandinista Revolution and Mass Democracy', *International Viewpoint* no. 76 (20 May 1985).

10. The two most prolific theorists of the participatory budget in Porto Alegre have been its two former mayors, Raul Pont and Tarso Genro. While Raul Pont's interpretation (see his contributions elsewhere in this book) presupposes a radical transfer of sovereignty to the population through new institutions of participatory democracy, Tarso Genro's is more nuanced, pointing to the PB as a way of 'restoring the credibility of the state'.

11. Fernando de la Rua was overthrown by the popular revolt of December 2001 after he had failed to deliver on any of his centre-left promises.

12. Most of the accounts and rumours attribute Celso Daniel's death to organised criminal interests – possibly drug traffickers or corrupt contractors in conflict with his administration – but there is little hard evidence.

13. *Governo e Cidadania: Balanço e reflexoes sobre o modo petista de governar* (São Paulo: Editora Fundacão Perseu Abramo, 1999).

14. 'Lula's Victory and the Trap of Participatory Budget', *Left Turn*, 29 October 2002.

15. See for example Salvatore Cannavò, *Porto Alegre capitale dei movimenti: Percorsi e progetti di un movimento globale* (Rome: Manifestolibri, 2002).

16. This tradition is particularly strong in the areas of popular education, popular communication and popular culture, which played such an important part in the Latin American left. See the work of the Uruguayan Mario Kaplun; Armand Mattelart, a Belgian working in Chile and elsewhere; or the Brazilian dramatist Augusto Boal.
17. See for example Robert Chambers, 'Rural Appraisal: Rapid, Relaxed and Participatory', IDS, October 1992, and a series of other IDS publications around this time.
18. See T.M. Thomas Isaac and Richard W. Franke, *Local Democracy and Development: The Kerala People's Campaign for Decentralized Planning* (Lanham, MD: Rowman & Littlefield, 2002), and Vandana Shiva, 'JAIV PANCHAYAT – The Living Democracy Movement', www.swaraj.org/Jaiv%20Panchayat.htm
19. See John Holloway, *Change the World without Taking Power: The Meaning of Revolution Today* (London: Pluto Press, 2002), and the enormous debate in response on the website of the Argentine Marxist journal *Herramienta*: www.herramienta.com.ar/

2   FROM FIRST STEPS TO FINAL STRATEGIES

1. Assis Brasil Olegario Filho is coordinator of Porto Alegre's community relations council. For biographical deals on de Souza, Passos and Pont, see their own chapters later in this book.
2. During the late 1970s and early 1980s, the Communist Party of Brazil (PCdoB) played an important part in several social movements that were mobilising against the military dictatorship, especially the movement of the urban poor. Brazil's populist movement, led by Getulio Vargas, was born in Porto Alegre and Rio Grande do Sul in the 1930s. It retained its strongest roots in that part of the country. After the transition to civilian rule, the Democratic Party of Labour (PDT) inherited the populist mantle, dominated many of the local social movements and held the Porto Alegre mayor's office immediately before the PT's election in 1988. Since then the PDT has had intermittent but unstable electoral alliances with the PT at national level and in some localities.
3. Alceu Collares of the PDT.
4. *Desenvolvimento humano e condicoes de vida em Porto Alegre*, PMPA-SGM, Porto Alegre, May 2001.
5. Sérgio Baierle, 'The Porto Alegre Thermidor: Brazil's Participatory Budget at the Crossroads', in Leo Panitch and Colin Leys (eds), *The Socialist Register 2003: Fighting Identities: Race, Religion and Ethno-Nationalism*, Halifax, NS, Fernwood Publications, 2002. This essay was originally a contribution to a seminar organised in May–June 2001 by Porto Alegre's then vice-mayor, João Verle, to discuss the PB's limits and propose modifications that might overcome them.
6. This is a half-humorous, half-serious reference to the Bolsheviks' call during the Russian Revolution for 'all power to the soviets'. Assis Brasil says that the United Socialist Workers Party, an organisation to the PT's left, initiated the call in Porto Alegre.

3   BASIC PRINCIPLES

1. An economist by training, Ubiratan de Souza was active during the military dictatorship in the Revolutionary Popular Vanguard, a guerrilla group operating in Rio Grande do Sul and São Paulo states under the leadership of Captain Lamarca, who was eventually hunted down and killed by the military. Banished from Brazil in 1971, de Souza spent time in Chile, Cuba and France before returning to Brazil in 1979. He was general coordinator of the Porto Alegre city hall's planning cabinet during the second and third PT administrations (those of Tarso Genro in 1993–96 and Raul Pont in 1997–98) before becoming general coordinator of budget and finances in the Rio Grande do Sul state participatory budget (1999–2002).

4   PORTO ALEGRE: THE CITY BUDGET

1. André Passos Cordeiro, economist, started working at the Porto Alegre mayor's office in 1995 and is general coordinator of the planning cabinet, which is responsible for the municipal budget, the multi-year plan, the budget guidelines law and the investment plan. Together with the community relations coordinating group, the planning cabinet represents the municipal government on the participatory budget council.
2. Sophocles, *The Theban Plays*, trans. by E.F. Watling, Harmondsworth: Penguin, 1947, p. 146.
3. The UN's Habitat II Conference in Istanbul, Turkey mentioned the PB in Porto Alegre in June 1996 as one of the world's 42 best examples of city management.
4. See Ubiratan de Souza's chapter later in this book (Chapter 6).
5. The 'city council' here refers to the conventional representative body elected in every municipality in Brazil every four years, along with the mayor and deputy mayor, as stipulated by the Brazilian Constitution.

5   THE PARTICIPATORY BUDGET IN TWO OTHER CITIES

1. Edinho Silva is a former minor-league professional footballer turned agricultural engineer. He is a member of the Socialist Democracy tendency in the Workers' Party (PT).
2. The Liberal Front Party is the main party representing Brazil's traditional oligarchy. It came out of the official government party under the military dictatorship.
3. After a particularly controversial privatisation process, Embraer became one of the few industrial success stories of the neoliberal 1990s in Brazil, selling its medium-size passenger jets to airlines around the world. The year before Edinho Silva became mayor, Embraer announced its plans to build a major new factory outside Araraquara.

4. Pepe Vargas, a doctor by profession, was elected PT mayor of Caxias do Sul for the period 1997–2000 and re-elected for a second term from 2001–04. He is a supporter of the Socialist Democracy tendency within the PT.

5. This idea of the educators being simultaneously the educated, and vice versa, is one of the core concepts in the 'pedagogy of the oppressed' developed by Brazilian educationalist Paulo Freire from the 1960s onwards.

6   ON A BIGGER SCALE:
RIO GRANDE DO SUL AND NATIONWIDE

1. 'Participatory management of public affairs – one of the hallmarks of our local and regional governments – should play a key role in reshaping the relationship between the Brazilian state and society, including at national level. The development of new democratic public spheres, directed towards public co-management and powersharing, towards a combination of representative democracy with participatory democracy, will also be a crucial factor in combating corruption, promoting rights and encouraging the participation of the majority of society who are currently excluded from almost all decisionmaking processes. It will open up not only space for state and society to debate and decide, but also a battle to displace the culture of political influence-peddling and the values of neoliberalism.' *Governmental Programme Guidelines*, passed by the PT XIIth National Meeting in Recife at the end of 2001.

2. Before being elected, Lula and his team promised to stand by the international obligations assumed by the previous government, including its agreement with the IMF. Very soon after taking office Lula's finance minister Antonio Palocci raised the target for Brazil's primary budget surplus to 4.25 per cent, even higher that that demanded by the agreement with the IMF. Later that year he promised that this target would remain in place for the rest of Lula's four-year mandate, thus severely restricting the scope for spending on social programmes.

7   PARTICIPATORY DEMOCRACY AND LOCAL POWER:
THE EXPERIENCE OF PORTO ALEGRE

1. This talk was given at the first World Social Forum in Porto Alegre in January 2001.

2. Raul Pont has been a leader of the left in southern Brazil for almost four decades. Imprisoned by the military dictatorship at the end of the 1960s, he became a founder of the Workers' Party (PT) in 1980 and has served on its national leadership ever since. He was the party's first candidate for senator from the state of Rio Grande do Sul in 1982. In 1986 he was elected state deputy and became leader of the PT group in the state assembly. In 1990 he was elected a federal deputy and in 1993 he became vice-mayor in the second PT administration in Porto Alegre. From 1997 to 2000 he was mayor of Porto Alegre and in 2002 he was elected again

to the state assembly of Rio Grande do Sul with the largest number of votes of any candidate.

3. Brazil's first constitution after the military dictatorship (1964–84) was contradictory. On the one hand it consolidated the conservative character of the transition to civilian rule, a process in which significant sectors of the oligarchy that had supported the military regime swapped sides in order to block any more radical process led by the PT and the mass movement. On the other hand it included some fairly progressive formulations and provisions, several of which (public service pension terms, for example) subsequently came under attack from proponents of the neoliberal agenda.

4. These 'municipal councils' are not part of the participatory budget, but are local consultative bodies already provided for in federal legislation and the Brazilian constitution to help formulate local policies in areas such as health, education and housing. For the most part they had never really functioned or had fallen into disuse. The PB in Porto Alegre helped to breathe new life into many of them, and in practice there has been considerable overlap with the work of the PB and its thematic plenaries (see Part II). One of the most successful, for example, has been the municipal council for the rights of children and adolescents, which has brought together hundreds of groups together to work on formulating local policies for children and youth.

5. In January 2001 Tarso Genro began his second, and the PT's fourth, mandate as mayor of Porto Alegre. In 2002 he resigned in order to stand for state governor and was replaced by his vice-mayor, João Verle.

6. The *'medidas provisorias'* used frequently by President Fernando Henrique Cardoso allow the executive to impose legislation by decree and only seek congressional approval at a later date.

8   THESES ON LOCAL GOVERNMENT AND THE STRUGGLE FOR SOCIALISM

1. Talk given at the second World Social Forum in Porto Alegre in February 2002.

2. The main debates at the second World Social Forum were grouped into four 'thematic axes'. Raul Pont contributed to a session on participatory democracy in the fourth axis, entitled 'Political Power and Ethics in the New Society'.

9   THE QUESTION OF DEMOCRACY TODAY

1. Raul Pont gave this talk at a seminar, 'Socialist Alternatives to the Crisis of Neoliberalism', organised in Porto Alegre by the PT's Socialist Democracy tendency after the end of the third World Social Forum in January 2003.

2. This talk was given less than one month after President Lula took office in Brasilia.

3. See note 4 in Chapter 7.

10   PT LOCAL GOVERNMENTS AND SOCIALISM

1. João Machado teaches economics at the Catholic University in Sao Paulo. A founding member of the PT, he was for many years a member of its National Executive Committee. He is the editor of *Em Tempo*, the newspaper of the Socialist Democracy tendency within the PT.

2. Similar concerns were present in other cities too. Luiza Erundina, shortly after she became PT mayor of São Paulo in 1989, said her administration marked 'the beginning of the social revolution in Brazil'. That suggests what the prevailing mood was in the PT's new municipal governments.

3. Although the PT as a whole supported the World Social Forum from the beginning, the real commitment to making it happen was always very uneven.

4. This chapter develops ideas contained in the text 'Atualidade de um Programa Socialista', presented by Raul Pont, Heloisa Helena, João Machado and Joaquim Soriano to the PT National Meeting in 2001. An English translation of that text is in the pamphlet *Lula President: A New Political Period in Brazil*, which Pont distributed at the third World Social Forum. While this chapter does not aim to make a balance sheet of the Lula government, which is still quite new, it clearly expresses a point of view very different from that which predominates inside the PT national government.

5. This should not be taken as referring to the Chilean Socialist Party at the time of Salvador Allende, which was not a typical social democratic party.

6. 'Soviet' here refers to the former Soviet Union, not to the soviets of the earlier revolutionary period.

7. 'National developmentalism' as well, though it produced several decades of rapid economic growth, never brought countries like Brazil real independence nor went beyond a limited form of bourgeois democracy.

8. In Brazil these privatisations were financed with public money through the National Bank for Social and Economic Development.

9. There are also false cooperatives, which are nothing more than a way for big companies to renege on their obligations as employers.

10. This perspective was clearly present in the programmatic texts adopted by the PT for Lula's candidacy in 2002. So far, however, it has had no clear impact on the practice of the new Brazilian government.

11. John M. Keynes, *General Theory of Employment, Interest and Money, Collected Writings Vol. 7*, London: Macmillan, 1973, p. 372.

12. What the neo-Schumpeterian school of economists calls a 'national system of innovation'.

13. This means that electoral campaigns cannot depend on marketing techniques, as has become common in Brazil even in the PT.

14. Historical experience to date is however not sufficient for us to tell exactly what form such a rupture may take in the circumstances of the new century.

15. This approach has similarities with Leon Trotsky's 1938 *Transitional Programme*, whose method was first discussed by the international

communist movement in the years following the Russian Revolution. The historical situation was very different then, however, in as much as the credibility of socialist ideas was much greater among wide layers of the population. Imagining a transition to socialism today requires a process that can restore that credibility. The question of how Trotsky's strategy then for a revolutionary break relates to the possibilities today of relatively peaceful electoral victories goes beyond the scope of this book.

Index